Rock Painting Fun
for Everyone!

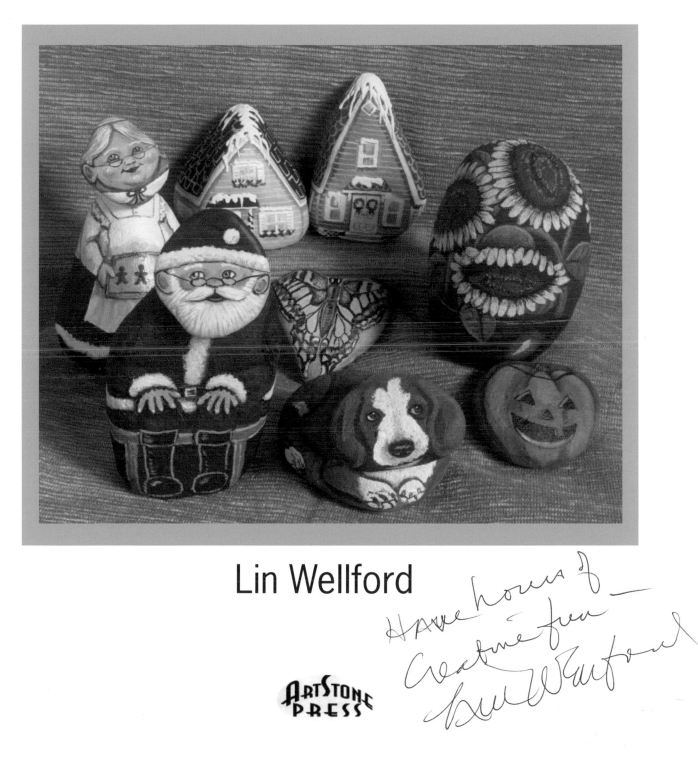

Lin Wellford

Have hours of
Creative fun —
Lin Wellford

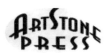
ArtStone
PRESS

Dedication- To Wandra Dees, Betty Haynes and so many other wonderful friends I've gotten to know through our mutual love of painting on rocks. Thanks for the support, the inspiration and the good times! Special thanks to Janell Robertson and Elaine Floyd for their help and advice. And, of course, to my husband Klaus for his patience and encouragement.

Other books by Lin Wellford:
Painted Garden Art Anyone Can Do
The Art of Painting Animals on Rocks
Painting Houses, Cottages and Towns on Rocks
Painting More Animals on Rocks
Painting Flowers on Rocks
Painting Pets on Rocks
Painting on Rocks for Kids
Painting Zoo Animals on Rocks
-also-
Paint Animals on Rocks with Lin Wellford-
available as video cassette or CD

Rock Painting Fun for Everyone.© 2006 by Lin Wellford.
Published by ArtStone Press,
210 E. Main Street, Green Forest, Arkansas 72638. First Edition.
Printed in the United States of America

11 10 09 08 07   5   4   3

Library of Congress
PCN 2005910687

Wellford, Lin
    Rock Painting Fun for Everyone!/Lin Wellford.
        p. cm
    Includes index.
    ISBN 0-9777065-0-8

Editor: Skye Pifer
Cover Designers: Lin Wellford, Skye Pifer, Kira Kupfersberger
Interior Designers: Lin Wellford, Skye Pifer
Editorial Assistants: Erika Kupfersberger, Kira Kupfersberger, Kristen Helams
Photography: Lin Wellford, Kira Kupfersberger

About the Author

Art, nature, and writing have numbered high among Lin's passions since childhood. Combining those interests into a satisfying career has turned into an exciting and unexpected adventure. Her previous rock painting books are considered a phenomenon in art and craft publishing, with nearly a million copies sold in the U.S. and in foreign editions. Lin has appeared on HGTV, MTV2 and Lifetime television and has been featured in numerous magazines, including Birds & Blooms, National Geographic's World, Grit, Artist Magazine, Family Circle Home Crafts and Painting Magazine.

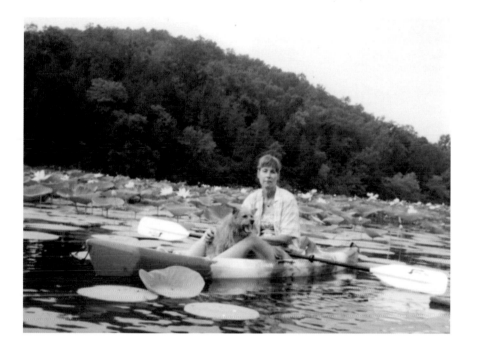

After publishing seven books with North Light Books, *Rock Painting Fun for Everyone* is Lin's first foray into publishing under her own imprint, ArtStone Press. She welcomes questions and comments and would love to hear from you. Email her through her web site, www.linwellford.com. Lin is the mother of three grown daughters and grandmother to Cameron and Catelin (so far!). She and her husband, Klaus, make their home on one hundred wooded acres in the hills of northwest Arkansas.

When not collecting and painting rocks, photographing or writing about rock painting, Lin likes to share her techniques and easy painting style through workshops and demonstrations. She also enjoys walking with her terrier-mix dogs, swimming laps at the community pool and talking family and friends into kayaking and camping with her.

Table of Contents

Introduction

Rock Painting Fun for Everyone takes the mystery out of making art. Like the fairy tale about spinning straw into gold, there is something magical about turning a commonplace object into a unique and appealing work of art. These pages are packed with projects simple enough for beginners but designed to appeal to more experienced artists as well. Easy-to-follow instructions and loads of photos guide you every step of the way. But why paint rocks? Rocks aren't intimidating the way more formal art materials can be. Even people with no art experience of any kind find that this is a fun and easy way to be creative.

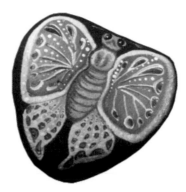

Painting on something that already has a shape is like discovering a shortcut to success. Just think of all the skills and practice it takes to create a lifelike image on a flat surface; foregrounds, backgrounds, perspective- no wonder so many people get nervous when it comes to making art! But none of that applies to rock painting. Simply choose a rock shape that suggests a certain subject and you are halfway there before even picking up a brush. The skills and techniques you learn while painting rocks can easily be applied to other kinds of art as well. People all around the world have shared stories about how rock painting served as the key that finally let them unlock their hidden artistic talents.

More Reasons to Rock

Other kinds of painting require expensive matting or framing before they can be displayed. Painted rocks are ready to show off as soon as the paint has dried. And rock art can decorate your world in a multitude of ways; on a desk top, mantle or hearth, on a porch, bookshelf or in a windowsill. Because they are solid and sturdy, you may use your painted rocks as doorstops, bookends or paperweights, even as jewelry and ornaments. Think of painted rocks as 'artwork that works'.

As you try your hand at painting your own rocks, keep in mind that you simply can not 'ruin' a rock! Just wipe off or paint over any mistakes. You learn far more from figuring how to fix those mistakes than you ever would if you got everything perfect the first time out. Creativity flourishes when you adopt a playful, fearless attitude.

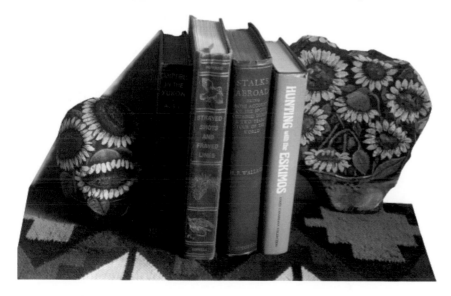

I wish you many happy hours of rockin' fun!

Lin Wellford

Getting Started- Supplies and Techniques

When it comes to inexpensive art activities, rock painting is hard to beat. Around the world there are rocks just lying around waiting to be picked up and painted. In fact, looking for interesting rocks and stones is as much fun as painting them! Once you become 'rock aware', you are likely to notice rocks wherever you go. If not, local sportsmen can often point you towards promising sources of rocks. Not all areas have rocks in useful sizes and shapes. In that case, check your phone directory under 'stones' or 'rocks' to find local rock yards. Such places often have a variety of rock types sorted into bins, and will usually let people choose ones they like and buy them by the pound at very reasonable prices.

Water tumbled pebbles are often sold in plastic bags at garden centers. You may not be able to use all of them, but there should be plenty of good ones to paint. Once your friends and family know what you need, they may begin to collect rocks for you as well.

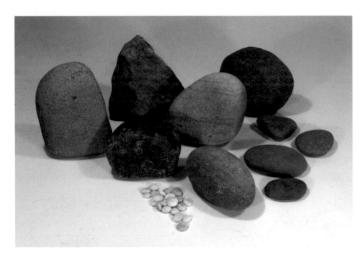

Here are just a few examples of the rocks you can use

Choosing Rocks

Smooth, water tumbled rocks are ideal for many projects, but several pieces in this book can be painted on what I call 'side of the road' rocks, that is, field stones or chunky rocks that have not been smoothed by water. In particular, houses and flowers are good subjects for these types of rocks. Avoid rocks with rough or bumpy surfaces that make it hard to paint details. Extremely hard, glossy rocks may require a base coat of primer like Kilz before acrylic paint will stick. Others that are chalky or sandy may not hold paint well, either. But that leaves many more excellent rocks, from bits of gravel, pebbles and flat 'skipping' stones all the way to baby boulders you can barely pick up.

Drawing Tools

To sketch on guidelines, use a regular pencil. White charcoal pencils are also good for drawing on designs, especially on darker surfaces. You can find them at art supply stores. Colored pencils are best for projects where darker lines might show through. Paint markers are useful for people who have trouble using paint brushes for fine lines. If you are not confident in your ability to copy designs freehand, you may opt to create a template by tracing any pattern onto heavy paper, then cutting it out and holding it against the rock as you draw around it.

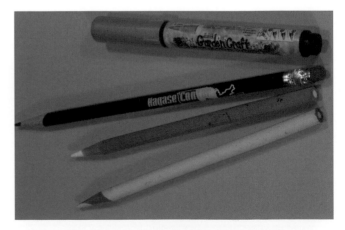

A handful of basic tools are needed for drawing on your guidelines or tracing around templates

Paints

Acrylic paint is easy to work with, inexpensive and readily available; perfect for painting on rocks. Because they may end up displayed outside, I use DecoArt's Patio Paint, an acrylic paint formulated to resist weathering. Then spray on Krylon clear sealer in a satin finish for more protection, and seal the bottom as well. Some rock types hold up outside almost indefinitely while other kinds seem more unstable and need extra protection. Of course, for rocks that remain indoors, any kind of acrylic paint will work just fine. Simply select colors similar to the ones I've used, and seal them for a more finished look.

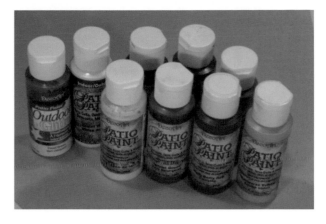

A small assortment of paint colors allows you to make just about any color you may need

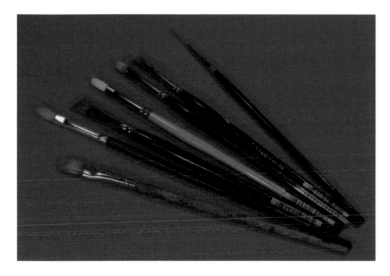

Narrow liners like the one at the top are perfect for details. Use wider, stiff bristled brushes for base coats

Brushes

Rocks can be hard on delicate bristles, so use bargain priced brushes with stiff, white bristles when possible. These are excellent for applying base coats to your rocks and although they wear down with use, they will still last through many rocks. For outlines and details, try Loew-Cornell's 7050 Script liner brush in 0 or 1. It keeps its narrow point and can carry lots of paint. Small and medium flat brushes are great for a variety of painting jobs. Use them in tight spots or turn them on their sides for heavy outlines. Angular brushes like Loew-Cornell's 7400 series in size 3/8 or 1/4 series are indispensable for flower petals. Other specialty brushes like spotters and shaders will prove useful as well. A handful of well-chosen brushes should be all you need.

Glues and Cements

Join rocks together to add even more dimension. Liquid Nails makes a clear adhesive that works well, but their original adhesive seems to hold rocks together best and comes in a 'Small Projects' tube for easy use. Wood filler like 3in1 Plastic Wood and Leech's Real Wood Filler are great for filling in cracks or holes in rock surfaces or to fix an unstable base. Wood fillers made with acetone, and clear cement also containing acetone, form a stronger bond together than either one does alone. When joining rocks, making a circle of the filler with cement in the center so that they mingle when the rocks are pressed together. Wood filler should come out thick like peanut butter. If it seems runny, insert a barbecue skewer into the tube and 'swizzle' the contents to mix them up.

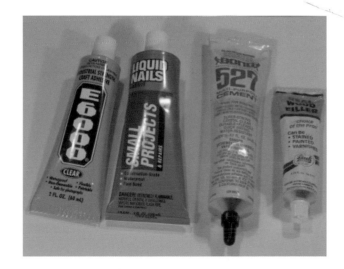

A selection of inexpensive cements and fillers will come in handy for your 'rockcreations'

Quick Painting Tips

☐ Cover your work space with newspaper; you can make test strokes on it while protecting your table top.

☐ Store-bought palettes can be used to mix your paints, but the plastic lids from margarine tubs also work well.

☐ Begin with a damp brush. This helps the paint transfer easily onto the surface you are applying it to.

☐ If you haven't used a brush before, you may be tempted to 'sketch' with it, lifting the tip with each short stroke. You will get better results if you place your paint-filled brush tip on the surface of the rock and pull out the stroke gently but firmly. The lines will be smoother and you will have more control.

☐ Some rocks are more textured than others. To get solid coverage, you may need to go back over areas to dab or fill in holes or surface imperfections.

☐ Anchor your little finger to the rock to steady your hand if needed.

☐ A long liner will carry much more paint than a short brush and save a lot of time.

Painting Basics

When painting lines and details, loosen up your paint with a small amount of water until you have a consistency that allows it to flow smoothly off the brush tip. Hold the brush nearly perpendicular to the rock surface to get clean, narrow lines. When lines look broken or fuzzy, the paint may be too dry. If lines fade as they dry, they were too watery. Avoid applying heavy layers of paint that take longer to dry and may create glossy patches on your rocks. Instead, use undercoats to help subsequent colors stand out or apply several thin layers, letting each coat dry in between.

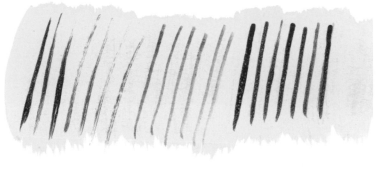

Paint too dry   *Paint too watery*   *Good consistency*

Mixing Custom Colors

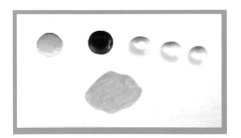

There is no need to buy dozens of different colors when it is so easy to mix just about any paint color you may need. The simplest way is to place small, same-size drops of the colors specified in the instructions onto your palette in a cluster, and then blend them together. To cover large areas, use larger amounts to ensure you mix up enough.

Create lighter and darker versions of the same color by adding increments of black or white to the original color, as I have done here with red.

Using Contrast

Contrast is a vital art element. In order to see shapes or details, there must be a way to 'decode' differences in any image we look at. Without contrast, it would be like trying to find a black cat in the dark! The strongest contrast is black against white, but contrast can also be established by using color variations. The two houses below show how darker and lighter shades of the same colors can be used to define shapes and add details. Learn to look for areas that lack definition and then use contrasting colors and lines to make the various elements stand out clearly.

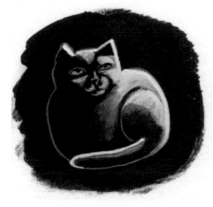

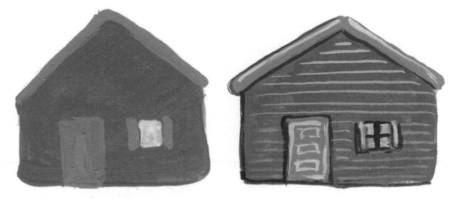

Without contrasts, this cat would be nearly invisible!

Colors that are similar need the extra help of defining outlines and details

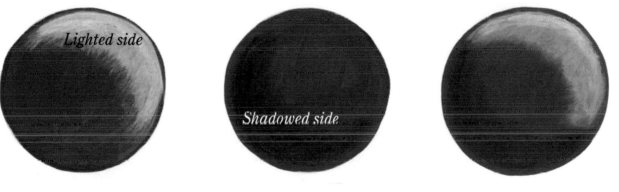

Creating Highlights and Shadows

Highlights and shadows help make any painting look more real. Even though rocks already have dimension, you can use the illusion of light and shadow to enhance the realistic look of your piece. Establish an imaginary light source and keep it consistent from piece to piece when painting rocks that will go together. Use white with a touch of your base coat color to create highlights. Add black to your base coat color to use for shadows.

Reconnecting with your Imagination

Applying Paint with a Dry Brush

This technique allows you to apply the paint for a softly diffused look with ultimate control. Pick up a small amount of paint on a stiff, slightly dampened brush, then wipe away most of the pigment so that what remains must be scrubbed into place. This technique is excellent for applying blushes and shadows to skin tones and for adding highlights and shadows to any area where you want a subtle, blended look. It is also easy for new painters as you need less hand-eye coordination to scrub. The result resembles airbrushing.

One last indispensable item for rock painting is your imagination. It's the part of your brain that used to help you see elephants and sailing ships in the passing clouds, and you can harness it again to help see the possibilities in the rocks you pick up to paint. Everyone has an imagination, but yours might need a little dusting off. Like a muscle, you will find that it becomes stronger and more supple with use!

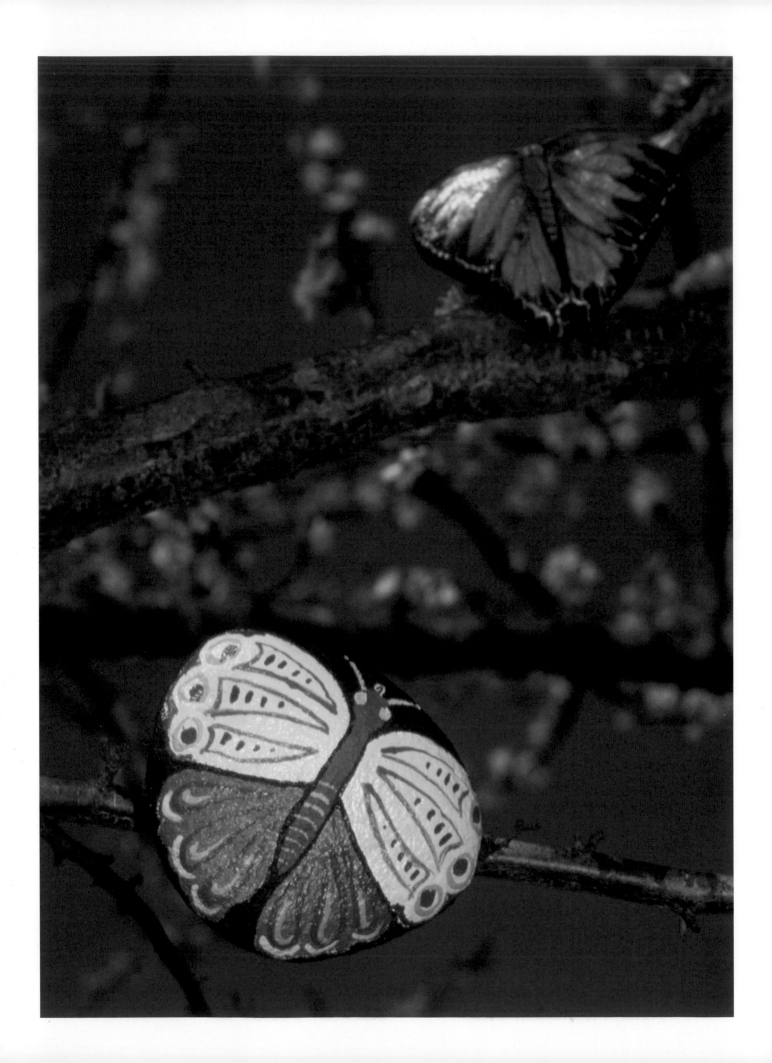

Rock Butterflies

Whether you prefer art that is realistic, fanciful or stylized, butterflies make wonderful subjects. Photographs can provide ideas about how to combine colors and patterns or you can just make up your own designs. Look for rocks that are fairly thin and smooth. Paint the wings spread fully, partially open or in side view.

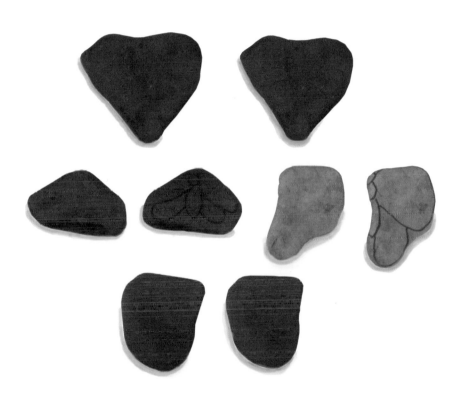

> ### *What you'll need:*
> - Regular graphite pencil
> - Red or orange colored pencil
> - Assorted brushes including small and medium shaders sizes 4 and 6, long liner brush in 0
> - DecoArt Patio Paint (or equivalent) in:
>   Tango Blue
>   Cloud White
>   Sunshine Yellow
>   Fuchsia
>   Tiger Lily Orange
>   Petunia Purple
>   Larkspur Blue

Pick a Rock

Add a basic design and any of these common rock shapes can be transformed into a butterfly that's ready to paint!

The rock I chose suggests an open winged pose. Make sure your rock is clean and dry before going on.

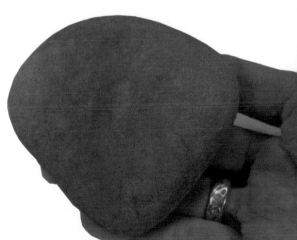

The blue butterfly in the photo opposite got its shimmer from a coat of iridescent nail polish

1 Draw on the Design

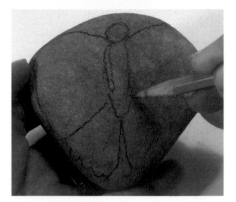

Use a pencil to draw two sets of wings, using as much of the rock surface as possible. Each side should mirror the other. I gave the lower wings scalloped edges.

2 Paint Away Excess Rock

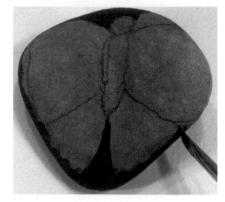

Dark shades of paint can 'erase' unwanted areas surrounding the butterfly. Use a shader brush to cover the outside edges so no plain rock is visible. Switch to a liner brush to outline around the body and between the wings.

3 Undercoat the Rock

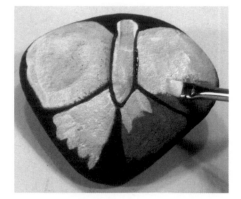

An undercoat of white paint will help subsequent colors look more vibrant. Let dry.

4 Paint Upper Wings

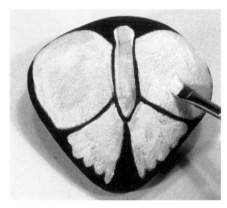

A bright color like Sunshine Yellow looks great. Use a small shader brush to fill in the upper wings.

5 Paint Lower Wings and Body

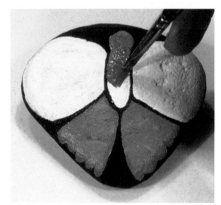

For a vivid pink on the lower wings and body, lighten Fuchsia with a trace of white. Let dry.

6 Sketch on Markings

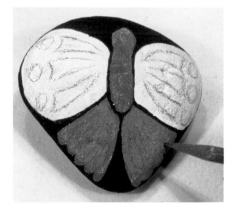

Use a pencil to sketch on the design or duplicate and trace over the pattern. Graphite lines may show through so use a colored pencil on lighter areas.

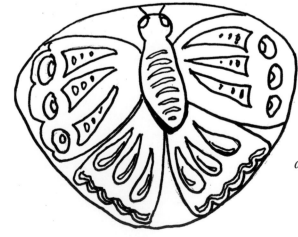

This stylized design is just one of the thousands of ways to decorate your butterfly

7 Paint the Markings

A variety of colorful details will bring your butterfly to life. Use a liner brush and loosen your paint slightly with water for smoother application as you go over outlines as shown.

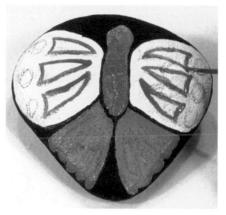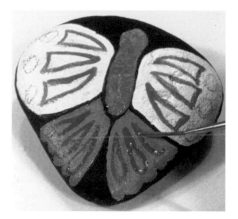

Use Tangerine Orange to outline the shapes on the upper wings.

Switch to Petunia Purple to outline the teardrop shapes in the lower wings.

8 Add Wing Details

Use a light blue like Larkspur to outline the circles on the upper wings and add a line inside each of the teardrops on the lower wings.

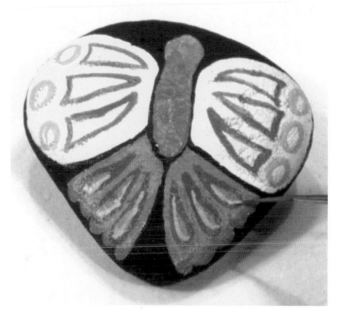

9 More Wing and Body Details

Give each blue circle a smaller center of Petunia Purple. On the head, create two round eyes and a set of feelers with Sunshine Yellow, then add yellow trim to the scalloped edge of the bottom wings. Make a row of curved lines down the center of the body.

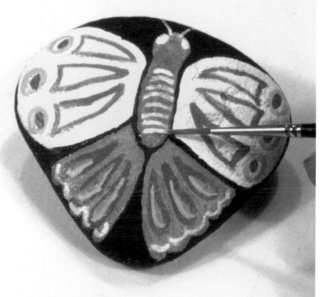

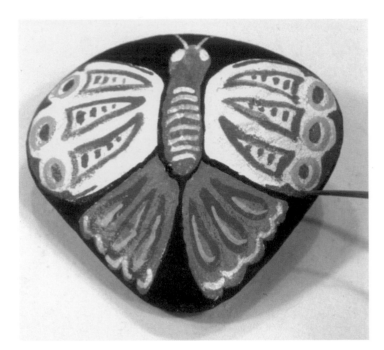

10 Finishing Touches

A set of Fuchsia dots decorate the centers of the orange shapes in the upper wings. Also use Fuchsia to add a scalloped trim along the outside edges of the upper wings helps pull the design together.

Other touches, like glitter paint and glimmering or iridescent nail polishes can also add glamor to your butterflies!

Protect and enhance your butterfly by giving it a coat of clear sealer.

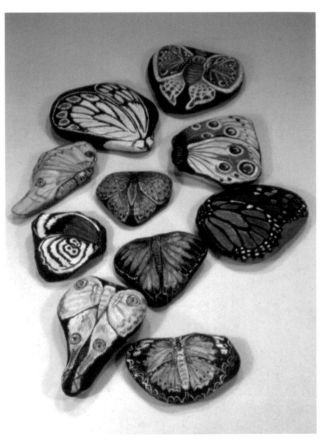

More Ideas...

Nature photographs are a wonderful resource to help you see how to match various butterfly species to a wide range of rock shapes.

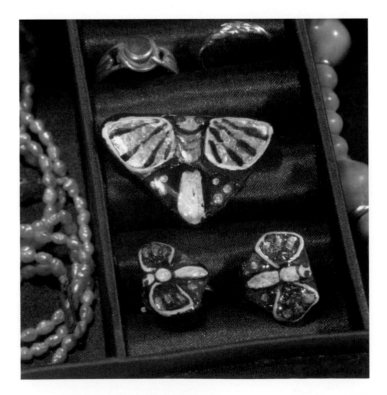

Make Jewelry!

I created this set of butterfly jewelry by combining regular and metallic acrylic paints with glitter paint and shimmering nail polishes. Several coats of clear sealer (I used DecoArt Paper Effects) give the pieces their enameled look. Pin backs and earring clips are glued on.

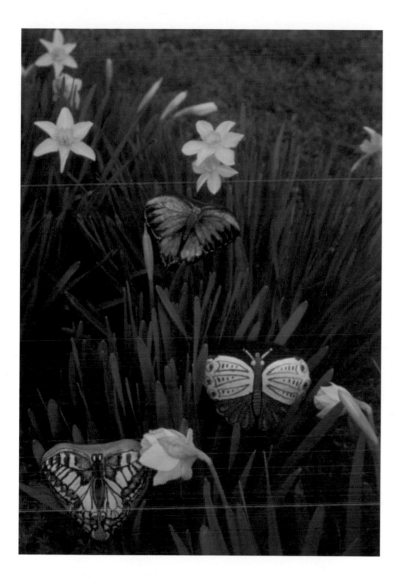

Create Colorful Garden Accents

Slender wooden dowels, spray painted green, were glued to the backs of these butterflies. When the dowels are planted firmly into the ground, the butterflies appear to hover among the flowers

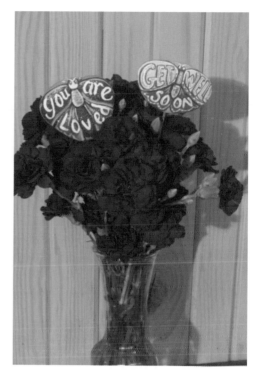

Whimsical butterflies glued to skewers can convey personalized messages

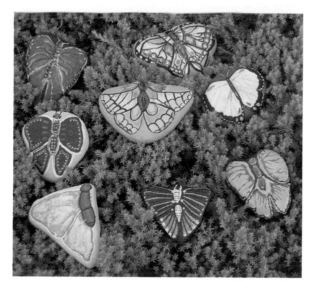

These beauties were painted by friends of mine at a rock painting party in Pennsylvania. Some are realistic while others are original designs, but each one is enchanting and unique

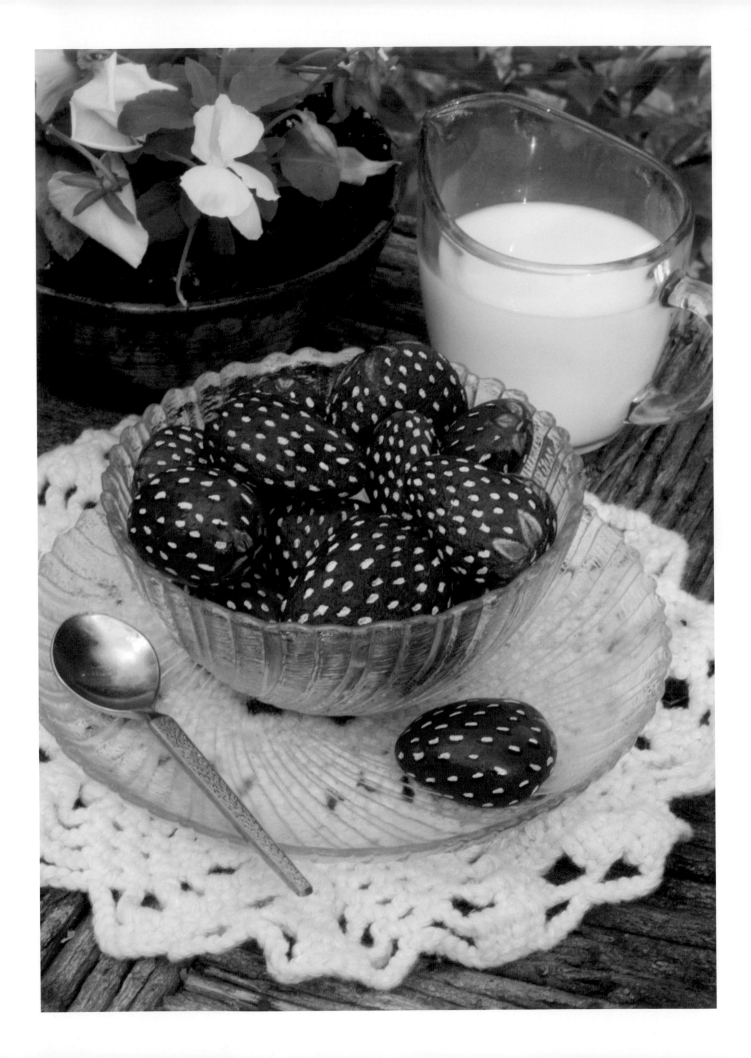

How to Paint

Stoneberries

A bowl of plump, ripe strawberries adds a springtime splash of color to any decor. The rocks needed are surprisingly common and the shapes don't have to be perfect, so it doesn't matter if your berries are more oval than tapered or a bit too angular. Paint may not stick to glassy smooth stones, so if yours are highly polished or slick, use a stain blocking primer like Kilz as a base coat to ensure subsequent layers will not wear off.

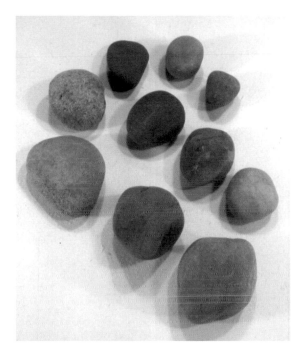

Strawberry stones may be as large as plums or as small as pecans. Choose a variety of shapes and sizes for a more natural look.

What you'll need:

- Pencil
- Assorted small and medium brushes including shaders in size 6 and 4 script liner size 0 or 1 spotter in size 0
- DecoArt Patio Paint (or equivalents) in:
  Cloud White
  Geranium or
  Holly Red
  Sprout Green
  Citrus Green
  Wrought Iron Black
  Sunflower Yellow

Choose a Stone

The rock I chose is an oval shape that tapers slightly. If you plan to paint more than one, set them up in assembly line style. Always make sure your rocks are well scrubbed and allowed to dry before painting.

1 Apply the White Undercoat

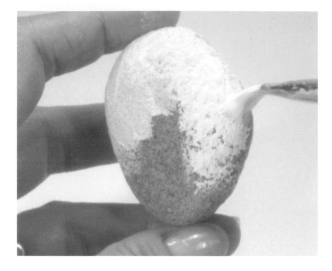

A light colored undercoat will brighten the subsequent base coat. It could be white or yellow.

2 Draw Leafy Cap

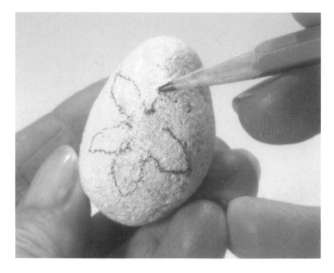

Use a pencil to draw on a star-shaped cap formed of five joined leaflets at the larger end of your rock.

3 Paint Red Base Coat

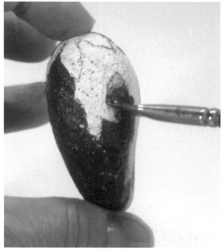

Cover all of the rock except the cap with Geranium Red. You may need to prop the rock or paint it in stages to avoid smearing the paint.

4 Paint Green Cap

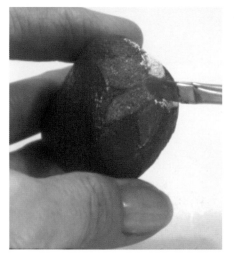

Use a small angular or flat brush to paint the cap with Sprout Green. Keep the edges smooth.

5 Add Highlights

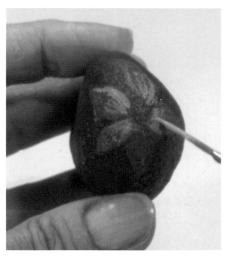

Switch to Citrus Green (or add yellow to Sprout Green) and use it to highlight around the base and along one side of each leaflet. Highlight the top of the stem to help it stand out.

Pattern for strawberry cap

6 Define Cap Contours

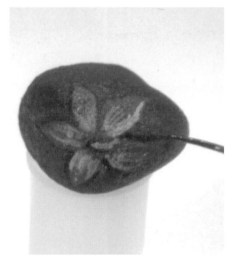

Darken Sprout Green with a bit of black and use this mixture to outline around the edges of the cap and along the stem on one side.

7 Create Seed Shadows

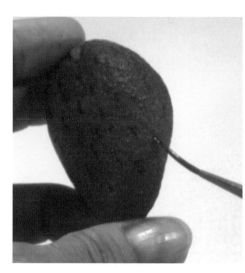

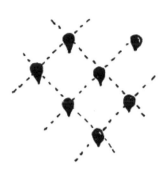

Place seeds in a roughly diamond shaped formation

Tip: Practice your seed pattern on what will be the back side first

Mix enough Wrought Iron Black into a drop of red paint to get a deep maroon color. Use the tip of a liner brush to paint small comma shapes. Space them as shown.

8 Paint the Seeds

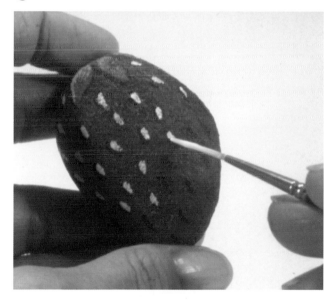

Add a touch of Sunflower Yellow to a drop of Cloud White to create a soft ivory color. Use the tip of your liner or spotter brush to paint an inverted teardrop shaped seed that overlaps the darker comma shape so that there appears to be a shadow along the same side of every seed.

More Ideas...

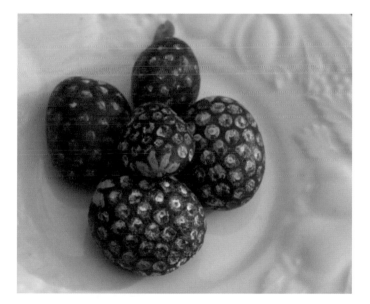

To make these berries, base coat each pebble in either black or deep maroon, then use Loew-Cornell's Berry Maker to cover the surface with pale grey or pale pink circles. When dry, cover with a watery wash of black or red, then use the foam tip of the Berry Maker to pick up the wet pigment in the center of each circle to create a soft gleam. Add a green cap when dry.

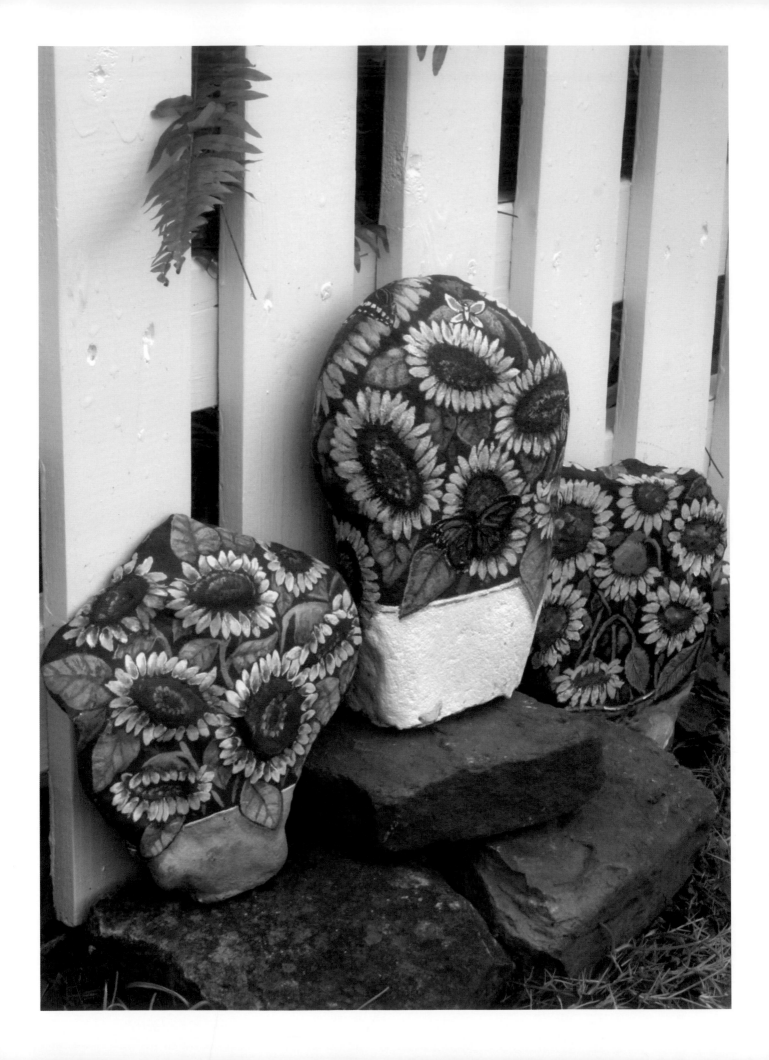

How to Paint a
Sunflower Vase

Big, bold sunflowers shine as brightly as their celestial namesake and have come to symbolize the warmth and bounty of summertime. Paint an everlasting vase of these flamboyant flowers and they will bathe any setting with a sunny glow.

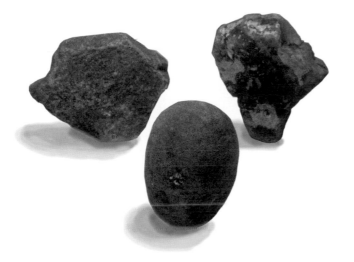

Sunflowers can be painted on a wide variety of rock shapes and sizes. Broken field stones work as well if not better than smoother, water tumbled rocks. Rocks that lack a flat end to stand up on can be painted for display in actual vases or flowerpots. Make sure the rock you choose is scrubbed clean and allowed to dry. Use wood filler to fix tippy rocks.

What you'll need:

- Regular pencil
- White charcoal pencil
- Assorted large and medium stiff bristle brushes Loew-Cornell 7400 series
  Angular brush in size 1/4 or 1/2
  Liner brush in size 0 or 1
- DecoArt Patio Paints (or equivalents) in:
  Sprout Green
  Wrought Iron Black
  Tango Blue
  Cloud White
  Sunshine Yellow
  Patio Brick

1 Divide the Rock

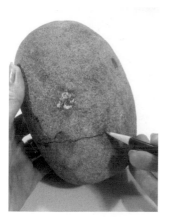

I chose a smooth oval rock with a flat bottom. The vase portion should take up between one fourth and one third of the total height of the rock. Use a pencil to mark the top or rim of the vase all the way around.

2 Paint the Flower Base Coat

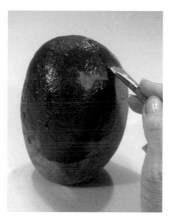

Combine Sprout Green and black 2:1 to get a very dark green and apply it to the upper portion of the rock with a stiff brush until it is solidly covered all the way around. Let dry.

3 Paint the Vase

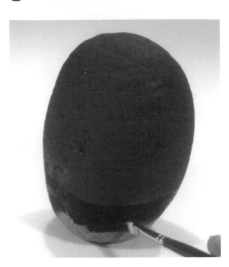

A blue vase sets off the color of the flowers. Use a clean stiff brush and Tango Blue to cover all the remaining visible surface of the rock. I usually leave the bottom of my rocks unpainted because I sign them there. Choose a different vase color if you prefer.

4 Detail the Vase and Add Highlights

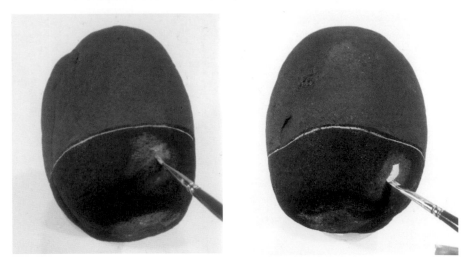

Add enough white to get a much lighter color. Use a liner brush to go around the entire rim just under the top edge of the blue so that a narrow line of darker color helps set it off. Switch to a larger brush and use the same light color, wiping off enough paint so that what remains must be scrubbed on, creating a smooth patch of highlight on the side of the vase. Let dry. Rinse your brush and pick up a bit of white. Paint a smaller smooth swatch of white in the center of the softer highlighting to create a bright reflection.

5 Layout the Flowers

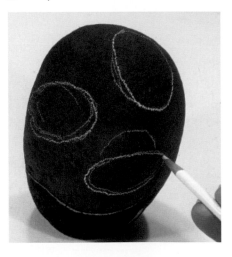

Set your flower centers in a triangular formation, with the roundest one near the top. Include one nodding flower and tip one in a different direction. For larger rocks you may need more flowers, but stick to odd numbers for a more dynamic design. Let the curves and bumps of the rock guide you in placing your flowers.

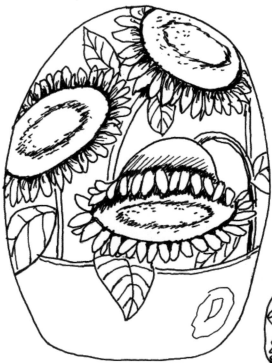

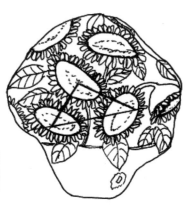

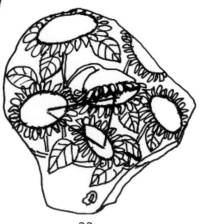

No matter what rock shape is used, create a focal point of three main blossoms

6 Sketch the Foliage

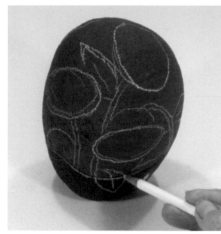

Fill the space around the flower centers with stems and leaves as shown. Repeat on the backside and fill in any empty places on the sides with flowers or leaves. Allow one or two leaves on each side to hang over the rim of the vase for added realism.

Tip- Painting over your white guidelines wherever possible will save you having to remove them with a damp towel later

7 Paint the Foliage

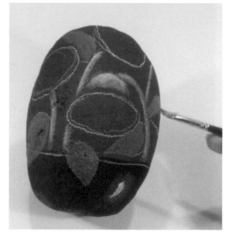

Use Sprout Green (or Pine Green lightened with Sunshine Yellow) and a medium size round or flat brush to fill in the stems and leaves, leaving narrow spaces of base coat between any features that touch or overlap.

8 Add Highlights

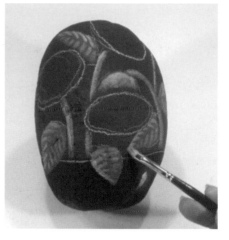

Lighten your green paint with Sunshine Yellow to create a clearly lighter shade and use this to highlight the curved top of the nodding flower and to highlight along one side of all the stems. Use this lighter color on the leaves to suggest segments, leaving the centers and veins in the original shade so that they contrast with the lighter areas. If the contrast is not clear enough, use some of the original base color to darken the veins.

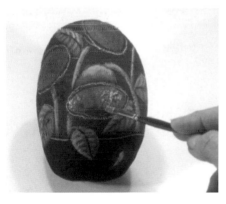

9 Fill in the Flower Centers

Use a medium stiff brush and Pinecone Brown to fill in the centers of all your flowers all the way around your rock. Leave narrow lines of dark base coat uncovered between these centers and any elements that they touch to maintain clear definition.

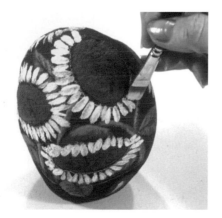

10 Paint the Petals

With an angular brush, place petals simply by lightly pressing the edge of the brush down, then lifting up. Use Sunshine Yellow to encircle the brown flower heads, leaving a narrow edge of dark base coat showing between them and the outside edge of the flower center. Vary the angles of the petals slightly with some narrow or partial petals between full ones. Petals should radiate out, each one perpendicular to the edge of the center except where they overlap down over the center on the drooping head as shown.

11 Repaint the Petals

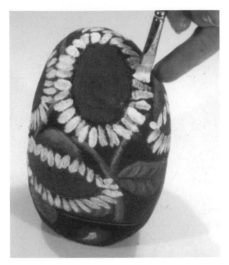

When dry, mix one part Cloud White with four parts Sunshine Yellow. Apply this brighter yellow with an angular brush, more or less covering each of the petals previously painted. Let dry.

12 Define and Detail Individual Petals

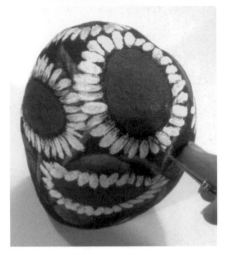

Switch to Patio Brick and a liner brush to separate and define any petals that overlap or touch adjoining petals. Also use this color to add a delicate fringe of reddish-brown lines radiating outward from the base of each petal all the way around.

13 Paint Dark Details

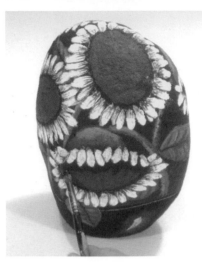

Mix Patio Brick with enough black to make a deep chocolate brown. Use a small flat brush or a liner to tidy and define the spaces between the petals at their bases surrounding the flower centers. Look for areas that are fuzzy or undefined and use this dark color to sharpen the contrasts. On the nodding blossom, create shadows directly below the overhanging petals.

14 Add Flower Details

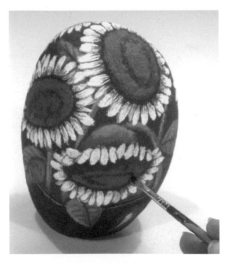

Use the same dark brown and the edge of a small flat brush to create a dark, ragged ring within each flower center as shown.

15 Finishing Touches for Foliage

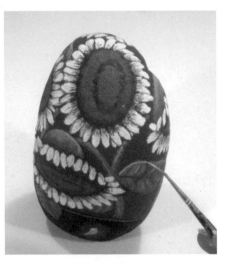

Tip- There is no 'right' or 'wrong' way to make art. Feel free to experiment and to develop your own style

Combine Sunshine Yellow and Sprout Green 3:1 and use a liner brush to lightly outline around the stems, the leaves and each flower cap that shows, ensuring that each of these elements stands out clearly.

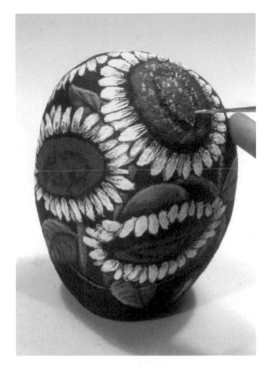

16 Finishing Touches for the Flowers

Rinse your liner brush and add a touch of Patio Brick to Sunflower Yellow. Use it to lightly stipple tiny dots around the outside edges of the inner circles on all the flower heads. Stipple more dots around and even inside the inner circle of any flower tilting upward where they catch the most light. Look for petals that seem ragged or fuzzy and use the dark green base coat color to redefine their edges.

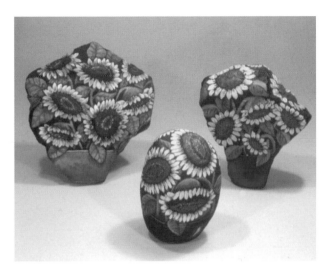

These are the same rocks that were shown unpainted at the start.

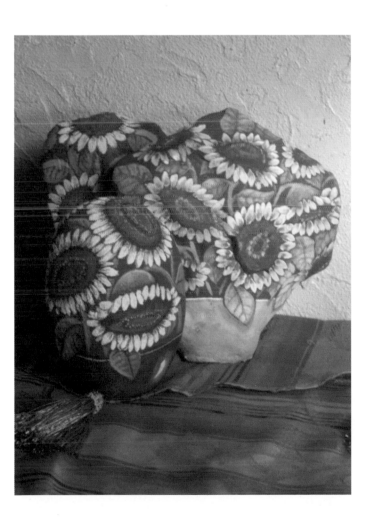

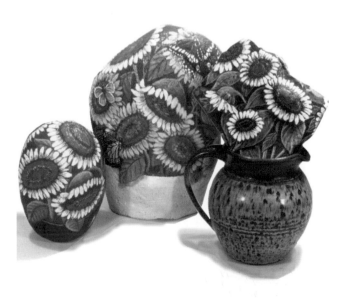

Cluster several pieces together for maximum impact. Gluing a square of felt to the bottoms of the rocks will protect furniture

Use actual pots or vases to hold bouquets that won't stand alone. Colorful butterflies can make a striking addition to any sunflower rock

25

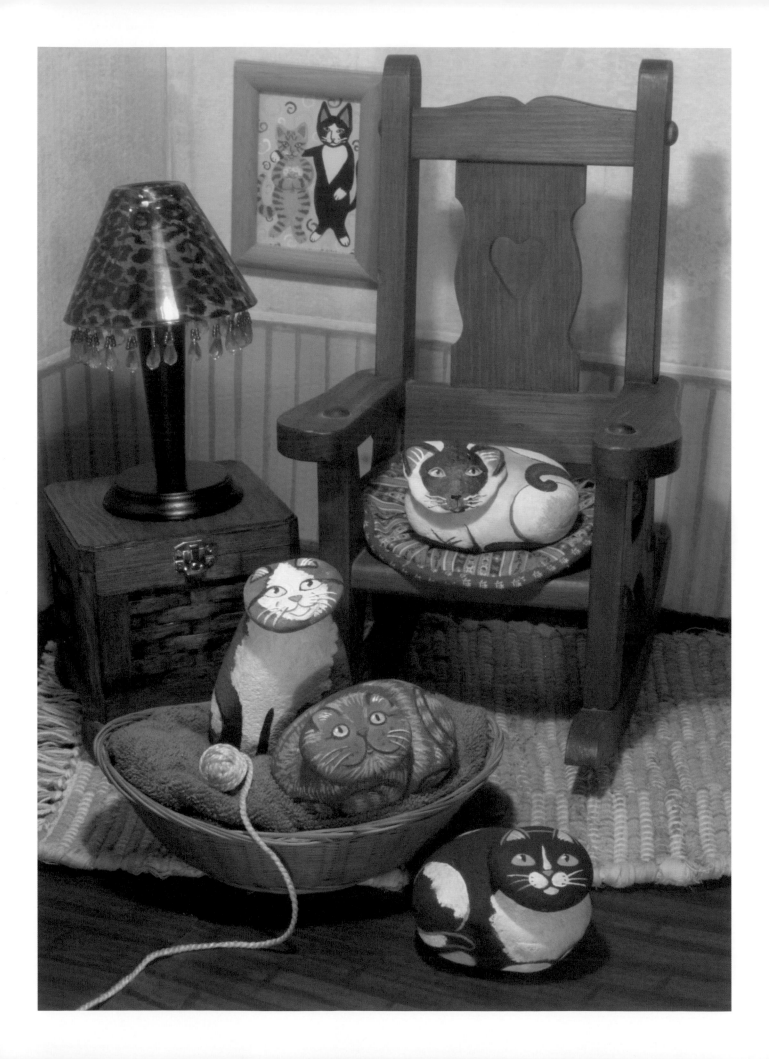

How to Paint
Rockitties

Create a charming piece of rock art sure to delight any cat lover. This simple design is easy to paint and the resulting cat has a stylized look with loads of appeal. Display several kitties together for even more impact. Or paint just the head and glue on a pin back to make jewelry that is the 'cat's meow!'

Select Matching Head and Body Rocks

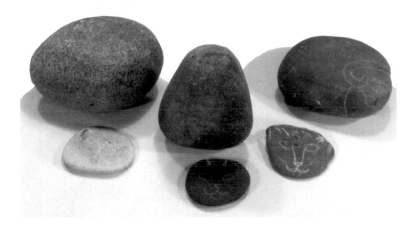

For best results, choose rocks similar in proportion to those above. The head may be round, oval or angular. For a curled or crouching pose, choose a body rock that is round or oval. An upright pose can be done on a more triangular rock with a flat base. When painting a group of cats, vary the poses to make them more interesting.

> ### What you'll need:
>
> - White charcoal pencil
> - Regular pencil
> - Assorted small flat or round brushes, plus liner brush in size 0 or 1 and a spotter brush or other small detail brush
> - DecoArt Patio Paint in:
>   Wrought Iron Black
>   Cloud White
>   Geranium Red
>   Citrus Green
> - Heavy Duty Glue

1 Apply Base Coat to Head

As always, the rock should be clean and dry. Use a size 4 or 6 flat or round brush and Wrought Iron Black to cover the entire front of the rock as well as the sides and any part of the back that may show when mounted on the body. Allow the paint to dry. For jewelry, choose a thin, coin sized rock for best results.

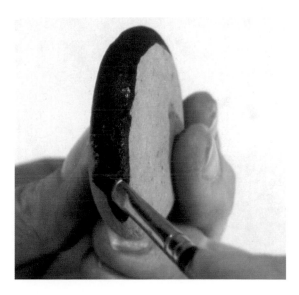

Cat face patterns

Persian

Siamese

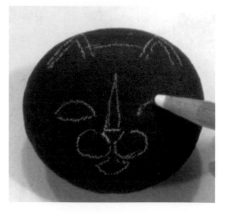

Use a white charcoal pencil to draw on the simple features.

3 **Paint White and Pink Areas**

Select a brush small enough to paint into small spaces. Use Cloud White to fill in the two round muzzle shapes, a small chin below the muzzle and a narrow streak along the bridge of the nose. Leave black lines between all the white areas to define them. Use the same brush to mix a trace amount of Geranium Red into a larger amount of white to get a soft pink. Use this color to fill in the triangle of the nose, leaving an edge of black surrounding it. The two larger triangular ear shapes should be filled in with pink as well.

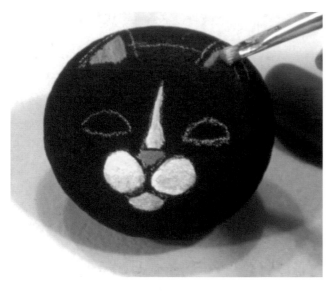

4 **Define Ears and Head**

Switch to a liner or spotter brush and mix black and white paint to make a soft gray. Outline around the outsides of the ear shapes, leaving a narrow line of black in place next to the pink. On either side and between the ears, extend short curved lines to indicate the shape of the head.

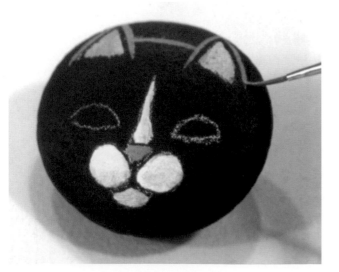

5 Fill in Eyes

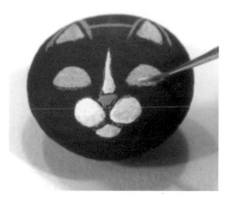

Use Citrus Green (or lighten any deeper green color with Sunshine Yellow) to fill in the entire eye shapes.

6 Add Details

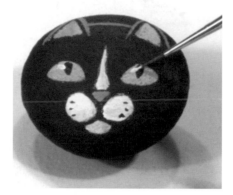

While eyes are drying, use a liner or spotter brush to add several black dots to the muzzle. Place narrow oval pupils in the eyes so that they extend down from the top. Switch to white paint to place a tiny dot of light in the same place on each eye.

7 Paint Whiskers

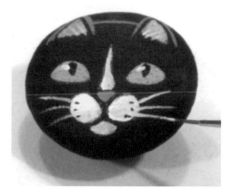

Use a liner brush and white paint loosened slightly with water, to add three delicate whiskers on each side of the muzzle. Glue a jewelry finding to the back and you can wear it, or paint a body to create an entire kitty.

Paint the Body

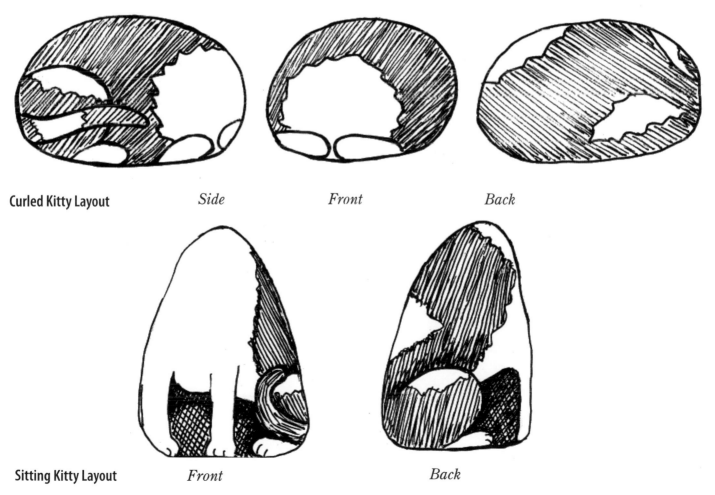

Curled Kitty Layout   *Side*   *Front*   *Back*

Sitting Kitty Layout   *Front*   *Back*

8 Draw Body Design

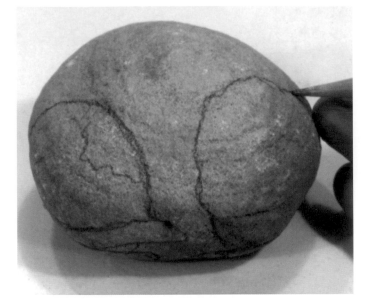

Use a regular graphite pencil to sketch round haunches at either side of one end of the rock. Curve a tail up from the end and tuck front and back paws along the bottom. Make a ragged patch on top of the haunch and a ragged circle that will form the chest and neck area. A white patch along the tail will help it stand out.

9 Paint Black Areas

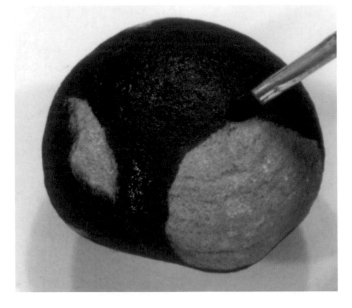

Cover the top of the rock with black paint. A medium, stiff-bristled brush works best. Leave the chest area, the paws, and the patch on the haunch and the tail unpainted. Outline around the edges of the paws to help define them.

10 Paint White Areas

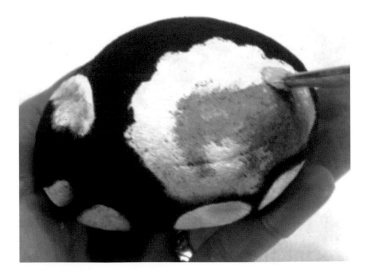

Let the black paint dry before filling in the white areas. When you are done, there should be no unpainted places remaining on the visible portions of the rock.

11 Add Gray Outlines

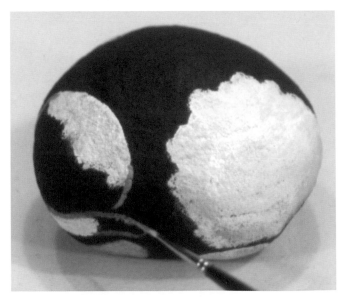

Mix a touch of black into a drop of white to make medium gray, and use a liner brush to outline the curve of the haunch and the shape of the tail to make sure these features are clearly defined.

12 Attach the Head

A heavy duty glue like E6000 or Liquid Nails will ensure that the head adheres firmly to the body. You may need to prop the body up with a small pebble to keep the head in position while drying. Allow adequate time for the glue to set up before touching or moving the piece.

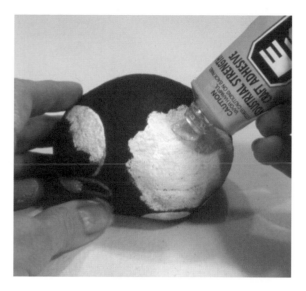

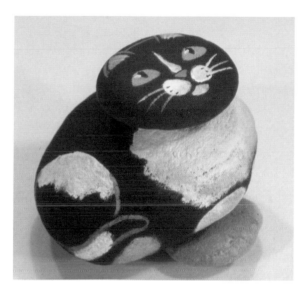

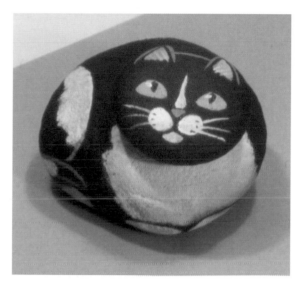

More Ideas...

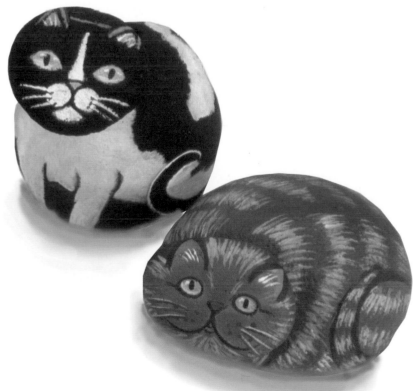

To paint a sitting kitty, use black paint to 'erase' the rock below the body and between the paws. The yellow tabby was painted by putting down a base coat of Patio Brick. Lighten Sunflower Yellow with white paint and use it to paint ragged bands of stripes. Make more delicate bands of fur lines with a liner brush.

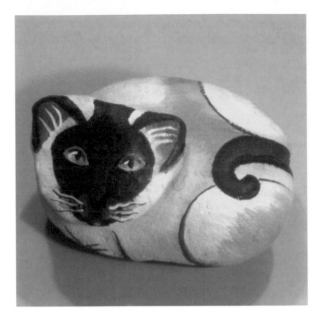

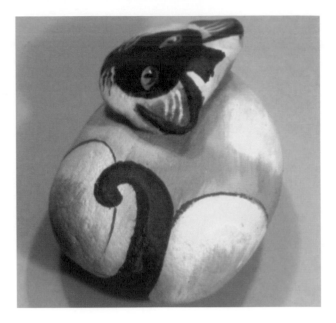

Create a Siamese by painting a white base coat. Use dark brown to outline the haunches, then fill in the face mask, legs, paws and the curling tail. Darken the brown with black and outline around the ears and the tail. Also use it to define the facial features. Mix 1 part brown with 4 parts white to get a creamy shade of beige. Use a dry brush to scrub this soft beige along the lower and back half of the haunches and along the back from behind the head. Fill in the ears with beige darkened with brown and a touch of red. Shadow and highlight blue eyes.

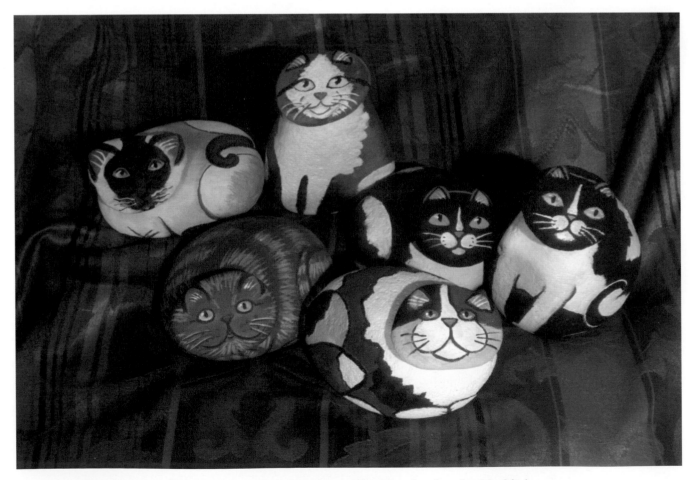

Painted pet rocks have personality plus (and no bad habits)

There are many other ways to transform rocks into cats and kittens. Here, instead of heads I added triangular pieces of gravel to give my cats ears that stand up. A combination of clear glue and wood filler, both containing acetone, creates a super-strong bond and the wood filler also covers up the joint so that it can be painted. The cat on the right has glistening eyes made by adding multiple layers of clear nail polish.

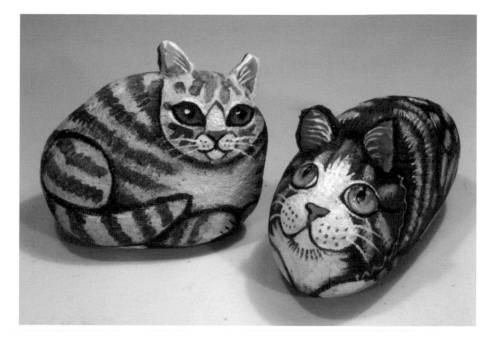

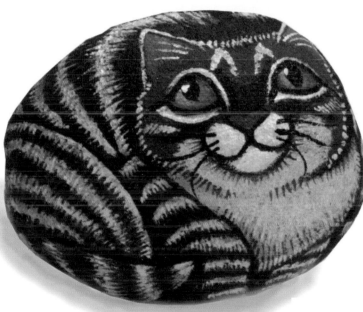

This cat is stylized but with more detail

With practice you may also want to try painting in a more realistic style. This cat has a dark brown (almost black) base coat which makes the lighter fur stripes and details stand out

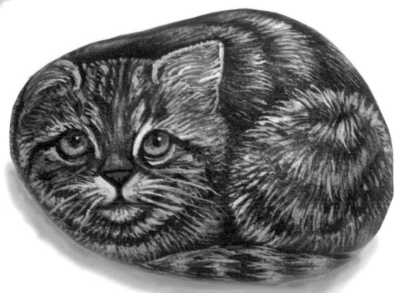

33

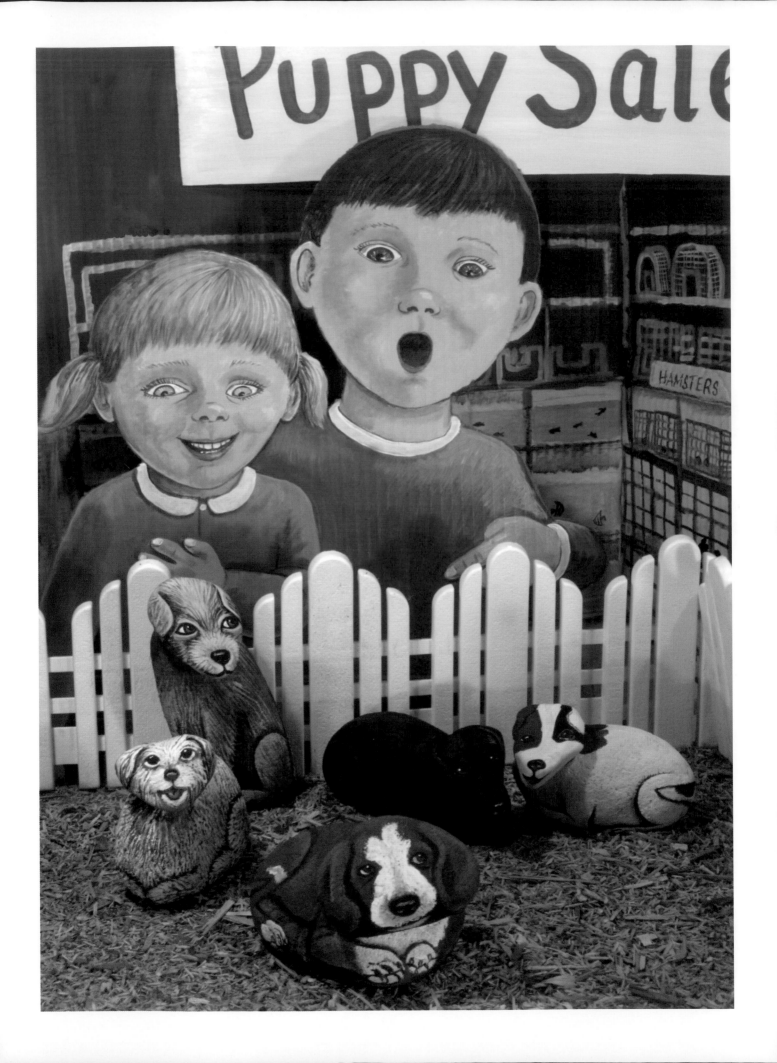

Rock Hounds

Could any dog lover resist these winsome pups? Combine two rocks to form a unique three-dimensional canine creation. Rock hounds are eager to go to work as decorative paperweights or desk art. Larger versions will happily serve as door stops or bookends. Different rock shapes, features and colors allow you to make a rock replica of any dog, whether pedigreed or mixed breed.

Select Matching Head and Body Rocks

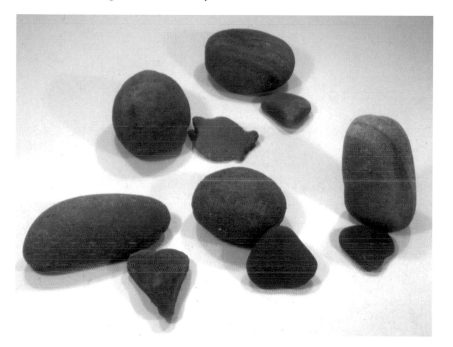

Each set will give your hound a different look. I chose a set like the one in the center for my rock hound.

What you'll need:

- White charcoal pencil
- Assorted small flat or round brushes
- Liner brush in size 0 or 1 or Spotter brush
- DecoArt Patio Paint (or equivalents) in:

  Pinecone Brown,

  Wrought Iron Black

  Cloud White

  Sunflower Yellow
- Heavy duty glue like E6000
- (Optional) Jewelry findings, paper clip or pop-top tab from soft drink can

---

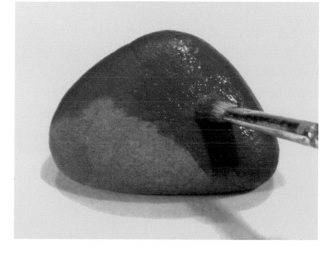

1 Paint the Head

Make sure the rock is clean and dry before covering all the visible surfaces with a coat of Pinecone Brown paint.

2 Draw on the Design

When the paint is dry, sketch on the features. Your guidelines will stand out better if done with a white charcoal pencil. Due to variations in size and shape, it may be easier to copy the design than to transfer it.

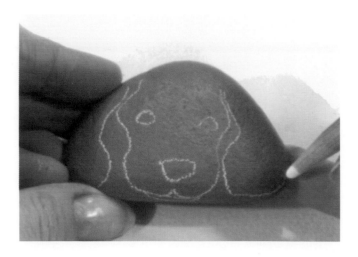

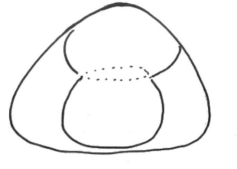

Establish head shape

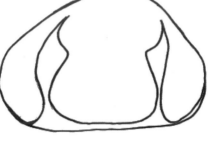

Add ear shapes

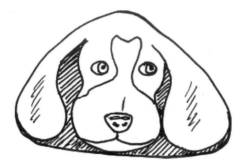

Add features and contours

3 Paint Contours and Features

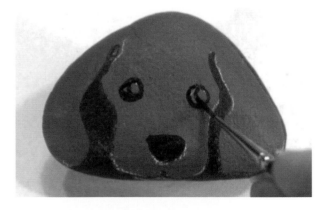

Soften black slightly by adding a bit of Pinecone Brown to it. Use it to outline the shape of the face. Also fill in the space between face and ears. Switch to black to paint the nose shape, to outline around the eye shapes and to add smaller round irises and pupils inside the eyes. Place them so that the dog seems to be looking sideways. Extend a line below the nose, dividing the muzzle area into two rounded areas. Add a shallow crescent chin below.

4 Fill in White Areas

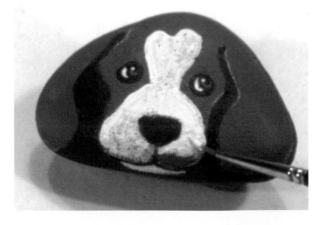

Use white paint and your small liner or spotter brush to fill in the slivers of white showing in the eyes along the side of the irises. Switch to a larger brush to paint the heart-shaped white face blaze between and above the eyes as well as the inverted heart shape formed by the muzzle on the lower half of the face. Also, paint the chin white. Add a tiny white dot in each eye so that they seem to sparkle.

5 Add Gray Accents

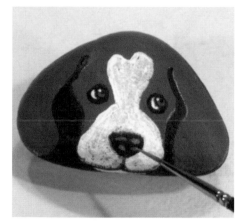

Mix up a tiny bit of gray by combining a small amount of white paint with a touch of black. Use this color to create a 'gleam' near the top of the nose, along with two partial crescents to indicate the nostrils.

6 Highlight the Fur

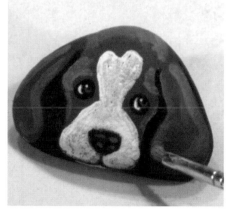

Combine Sunflower Yellow and Pinecone Brown 2:1. Pick it up with a small round or flat brush then wipe most off again. Use this dry brush to apply soft highlights to the top of the head and to outline all brown areas as shown.

7 Darken Ear Folds

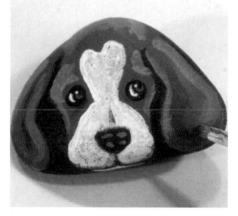

Mix Pinecone Brown with a bit of black to create a deeper brown. Add a small line just above the nose to suggest the length of the muzzle, then wipe your brush and apply what remains to the centers of the ears. The head is now done.

Create a Body for Your Hound

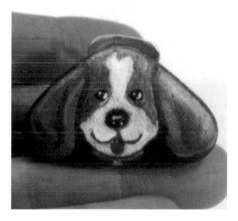

Art You Can Wear!

Lightweight rocks can be turned into pendants or other pieces of wearable art. Glue a paper clip or tab from a soda can to the back to make a pendant. Pin backs (available at craft stores) can also be glued on, but only very thin rocks are light enough to pin to clothing.

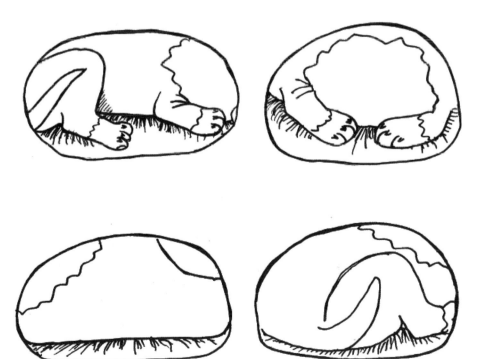

Many sizes and shapes will work, but a plump round rock allows room for a pillow your pooch can curl up on

8 Draw on the Design

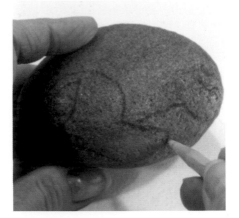

Use a pencil to sketch the body's features. If your rock is not rounded enough, leave out the pillow and straighten the angle of the feet and paws so that they are even with the rock's base.

9 Paint the Pillow

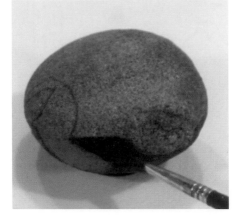

Choose your pillow color and apply it below and around the dog's body using a brush sized to fit into the tighter areas. I used Geranium Red.

10 Paint the Body

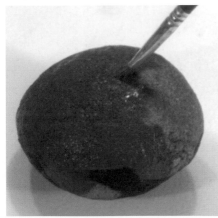

Rinse the same brush or use one slightly larger to paint the dog's body, leaving only the paws and the chest area unpainted. Leave the guidelines uncovered.

11 Paint White Areas

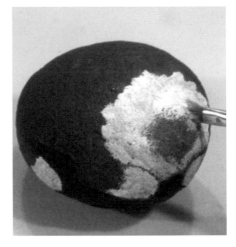

Switch to white paint and fill in the chest and the paws, leaving the guideline between the chest and paws uncovered.

12 Go Over Outlines

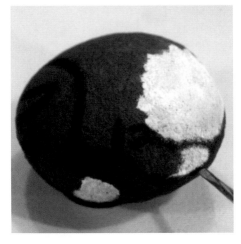

Darken Pinecone Brown with enough black paint to get a very deep brown. Use the side of a small flat brush to define all the contours clearly. Add a wedge of shadow in the angle where the back leg overlaps the tummy.

13 Paint Paw Details

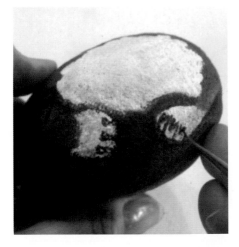

Change to a liner brush to add delicate details to the front and back paws as shown.

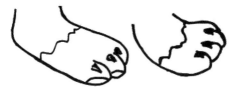

Details for back and front paws

14 Add Fur Highlights

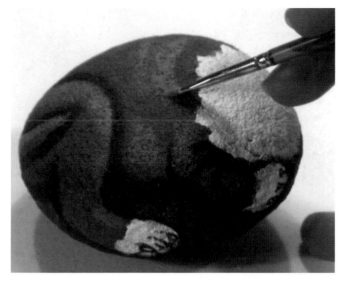

Lighten Pinecone Brown with Sunflower Yellow. Wipe away excess paint, then scrub on highlights along the top of the haunch, the top of the tail and the tops of the rear and front legs (on the brown areas only). Add soft highlights to the center of the tummy and create soft curves of highlights along the shoulders as shown.

15 Paint Pillow Details

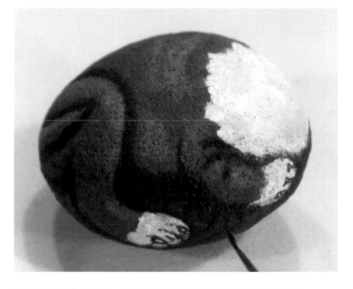

Darken the color used for your pillow with a bit of black. Remove excess paint so that you can dry-brush soft shadows in the areas where the dog's body meets the pillow. Switch to a liner brush and add a few longer lines of this darker color to suggest folds in the fabric of the pillow.

16 Attach the Head

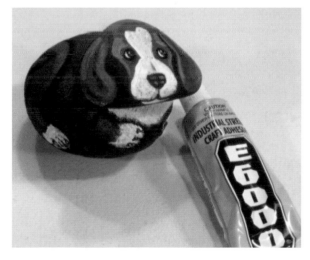

Use glue to join head and body. A heavy duty product like E6000 or Liquid Nails will make a sturdy bond. Experiment with placement to achieve a pose you like. Allow the glue to set up before moving the piece. Propping up the body so the head remains level will keep it from slipping out of position as it dries.

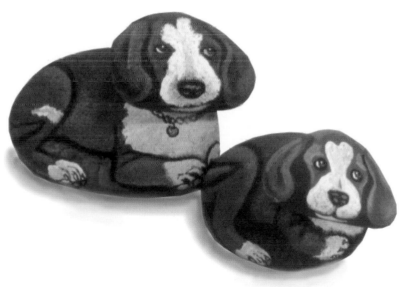

Paint a pair! I gave the larger rock hound a patch of white on his haunch, a blue cushion and painted a collar and tag

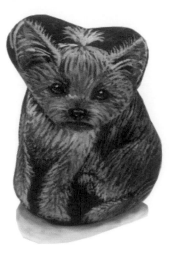 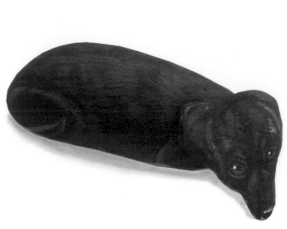 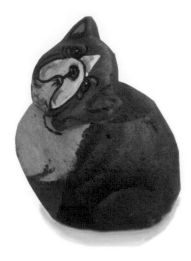

Dogs with upright ears can be a challenge. This yorkie has a heart-shaped head that gave me room for both ears and a little 'sprout' on top.

My dachshund was painted in black with rusty brown points. I used a mix of blue-gray to create the highlights that suggest contour and texture.

The head for this bulldog was a real find because it came with two points perfect for upright ears. The bulldog's shape and facial features differ from my hound's, but the colors used were the same.

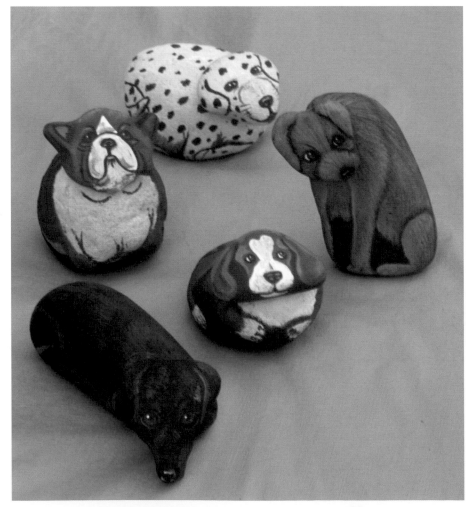

Select and combine rocks to suggest almost any breed in a variety of poses. The dogs below are the same ones that were shown as unpainted sets at the beginning of this chapter. They make wonderful gifts, keepsakes or memorials to celebrate beloved pets no longer with us.

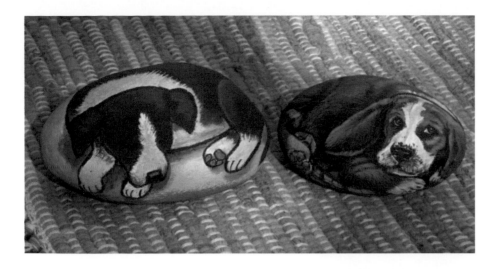

Another option is to paint your rock hound on a single rock. The one on the left is more stylized while the other was painted to look more realistic. As you become more experienced, you may want to try painting pieces that look more real.

Instead of a separate rock head, I added two oversized triangular rock ears (gravel pieces found in my driveway) to this chihuahua. To help the rock stand up, I also glued a small round pebble to one front paw, combined with wood filler to cover and smooth the joint. When painted, such additions will look like part of the original rock.

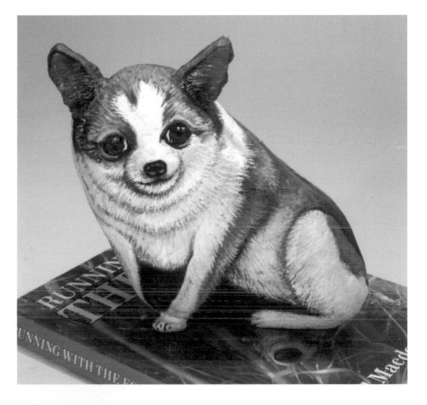

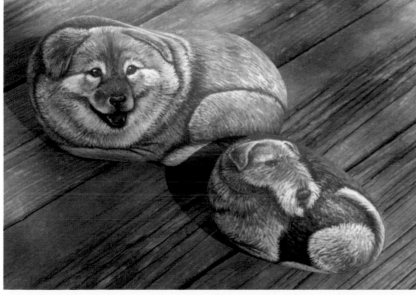

People love to have portraits of their pets painted on rocks. Working from photos is a great way to learn new skills

41

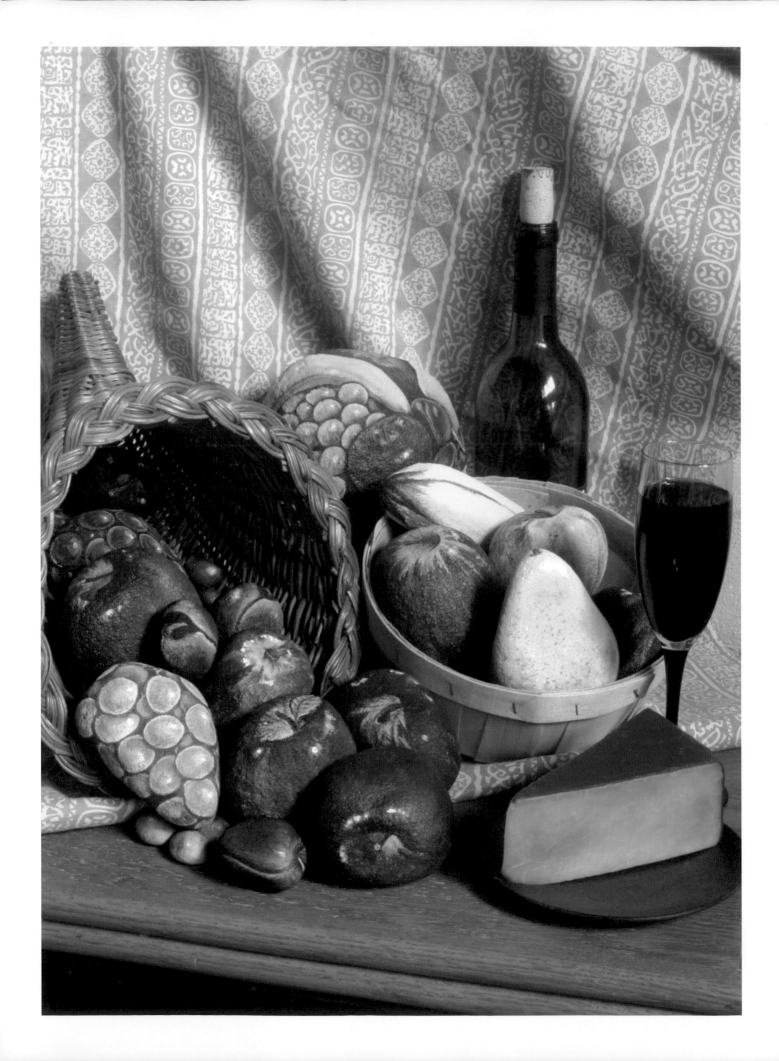

How to Paint
Fancy Fruit Rocks

Who says trompe l'oeil is just for walls? A layer of paint can transform rocks into fruit so sumptuous and life-like you'll be tempted to take a bite! Gather up an assortment of rock shapes and sizes and create a stunning three dimensional still life display for your tabletop. Add candles and evergreen boughs for holiday decorating.

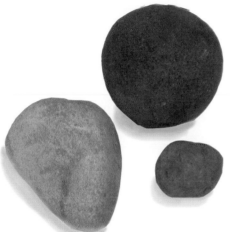

Select Rocks

To achieve realistic results, select individual rocks that are in proportion to one another. Apple rocks should be plump but they don't have to be perfectly round to look convincing. Grapes work well in a wedge shape and plums are small ovals.

Paint a Red Apple

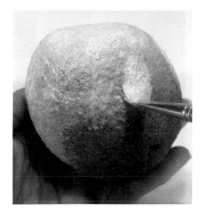

1 Paint the Undercoat

Use a large, stiff brush to apply a coat of Sunshine Yellow to the entire surface of your apple to help subsequent colors stand out. Paint one end first then set the rock on small plastic bottle cap while you cover the rest. For rocks that are naturally dark, a second coat of yellow may be needed for solid coverage. Let dry

2 Draw Stem and Rim

Use a pencil to draw the slightly tilted stem and a curved horizontal line indicating the rim surrounding the depression where the stem originates.

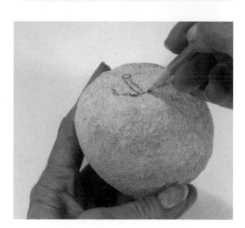

What you'll need for Apples:

- Pencil
- Assorted brushes including small and medium stiff flat brushes, small angular brush and a liner brush in size 0 or 1
- DecoArt Patio Paint (or equivalents) in:
  Sunshine Yellow
  Geranium Red
  Wrought Iron
  Black
  Cloud White
  Citrus Green
  Patio Brick

3 Paint the Top and Sides

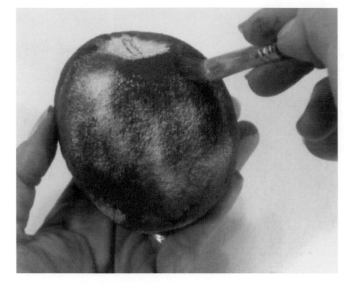

Loosen red paint slightly with water and use a stiff bristled flat brush to paint around the stem oval at the top. Stroke outward to cover the shoulders solidly, then make more irregular streaks on the sides, leaving small strips and patches of yellow showing through, especially in the upper half.

4 Paint the Bottom

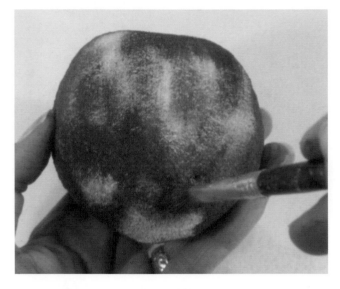

Apply red paint more solidly around the bottom, surrounding a scalloped opening of yellow. Add a few more streaks of red that extend up from the bottom. The overall effect should be pleasingly random. Wipe off excess paint then use the dry brush to soften the edges of your streaks.

Color Swatches for Apple

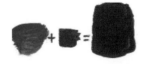

Geranium Red plus Black for darker streaks

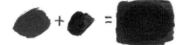

Patio Brick plus Black for stem color

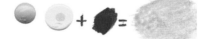

Citrus Green, Sunshine Yellow and Geranium Red for top oval

Combine watered down stem color with Sunshine Yellow for shadow

5 Add Darker Streaks and Transparent Red

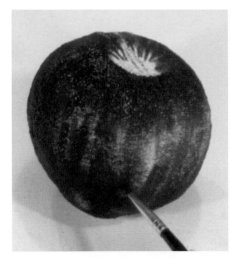

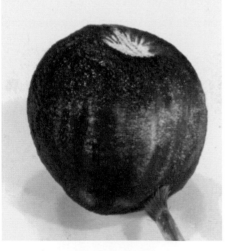

Use a smaller, stiff-bristled flat brush. Create a deep maroon color by adding black to red. Paint a fringe of small strokes along the far edge of the top oval. Deepen the top curves then layer and blend streaks of varying widths that extend down along the sides of the apple.

Switch to a larger brush and use a watery wash of plain red to blend and unify the surface with this transparent layer. Leave traces of the lighter patches showing, particularly along a raggedly horizontal band just below the dark shoulders.

6 Paint Top Oval

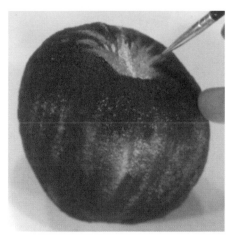

Combine colors as shown in the swatches to fill in the stem oval. Use a small angular or flat brush to paint the area on either side of the stem quite solidly, then feather narrow strokes of this color outward in varying lengths around and above the top of the stem.

7 Fill in the Stem

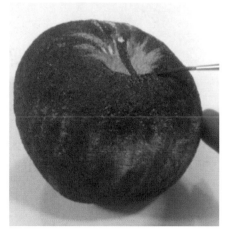

Mix Patio Brick and black to duplicate the stem swatch. Use a liner brush to paint the stem, leaving a tiny oval at the top outlined but unpainted. Add a line of this dark brown to the half-round rim below the stem for added emphasis.

8 Add Stem Shadow

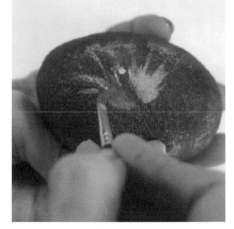

A hint of shadow to the left of the stem enhances the illusion of dimension. Use the stem color, but water it down to a light wash and add a hint of Sunshine Yellow. Apply with a small round brush, blending and softening the edges.

9 Finishing Touches

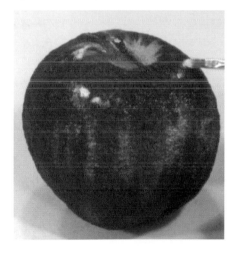

Soften any streaks and patches that seem unfinished with watery washes of red or maroon. Gleams of white paint give your apple its shine. Choose two or three areas along the shoulders and apply several slightly watered-down patches. When dry, place smaller dabs of undiluted white on top of the larger, more transparent ones.

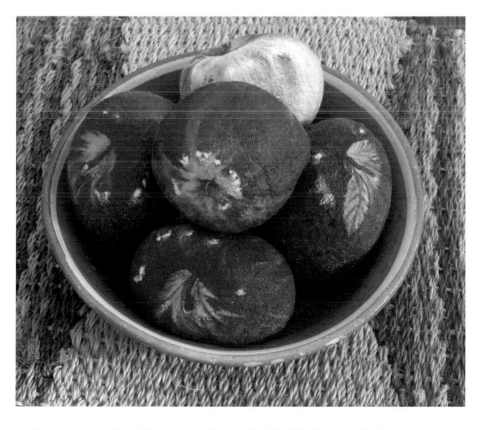

Seal your apple with a coat of clear finish like DecoArt's Americana Gloss Varnish or spray on several coats of acrylic sealer.

Paint Green Grapes

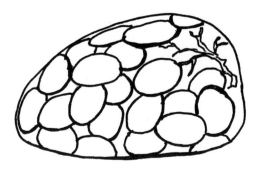

A plump rock with a somewhat triangular shape is perfect for painting a cluster of grapes. Scrub your rock and allow it to dry.

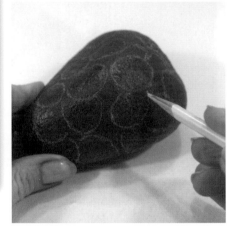

1 Paint Base Coat and Sketch Grapes Shapes

Using Pine Green or a mixture of Sprout Green and black (match color swatch on following page), cover the entire rock surface with a large, stiff brush. When dry, use a yellow pencil to sketch a group of marble-sized oval grape shapes set at varying angles along the top. Continue to cover the surface with overlapped ovals as shown. Fill in large gaps with partial ovals as needed. The cluster will look more natural if it is not too regimented. Leave a bit of open space at the wide end of the cluster where the stem will go.

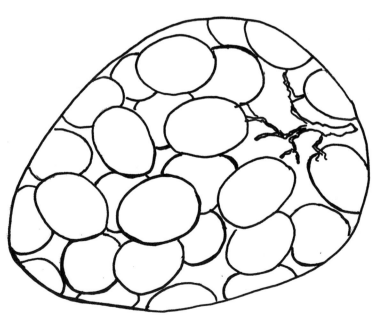

Top View

Side View

Patterns for Grape Placement

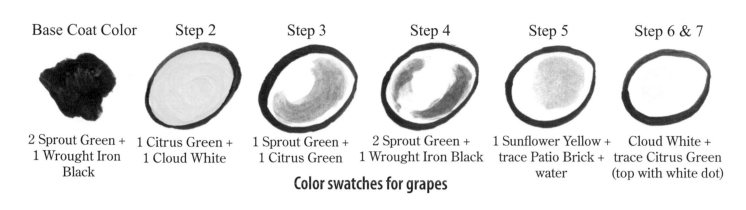

Base Coat Color	Step 2	Step 3	Step 4	Step 5	Step 6 & 7
2 Sprout Green + 1 Wrought Iron Black	1 Citrus Green + 1 Cloud White	1 Sprout Green + 1 Citrus Green	2 Sprout Green + 1 Wrought Iron Black	1 Sunflower Yellow + trace Patio Brick + water	Cloud White + trace Citrus Green (top with white dot)

Color swatches for grapes

2 Paint Grape Shapes

Match the color shown for Step 2. Use a small flat or angular brush to fill in the oval shapes, leaving narrow lines of dark base coat surrounding each one as shown. Fill in the shapes with circular strokes.

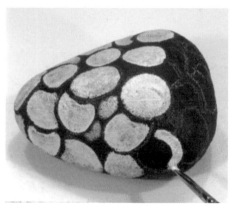

3 Add Contours

Mix the color for Step 3 and use it to add half circles of contouring shadows inside each oval. Also add green shadows below any grape that is overlapped by another.

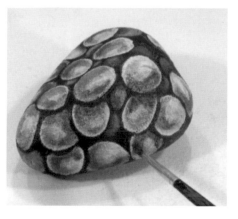

4 Add Darker Shadows

Intensify the contrasts further by layering on smaller, darker curves of shadowing using the color for Step 4. Keep your brush dry so that the shadows are soft and diffused. Add them along the lower edges of the previous shadows on the full grapes, and use them to deepen the shadows on the partial grapes. Leave at least a narrow outline of lightest green uncovered around the edges of each grape.

5 Apply Subtle Tint

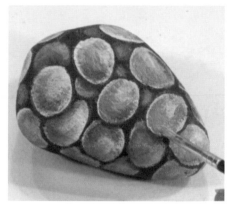

A hint of a warmer color gives even more realism to the look of your grapes. Apply grape color #5 with a wet brush so that it goes on as a transparent tint in the lower center of all the whole and nearly whole grapes.

6 Paint Soft Gleams

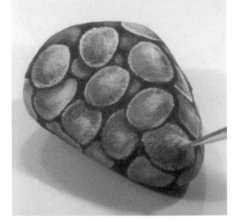

Soften a drop of white with a touch of Citrus Green and use a dry brush with most of the paint wiped away to apply soft circular highlights to the upper center of each of the whole and almost whole grapes.

7 Add Highlights

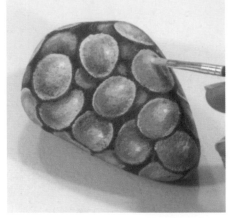

Switch to pure white to add a smaller, more intense highlight near the center of each of the softer gleams.

8 Paint the Stem

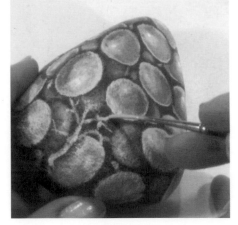

At the wider end of the rock, create a main stem with several smaller, slightly knobby stems branching off it to the nearest grapes. Mix Sunflower Yellow with a touch of Patio Brick to get a tan color and use a liner brush to paint these stem lines. Add white to the mix and use to highlight stem edges and knobs.

Paint a Purple Plum

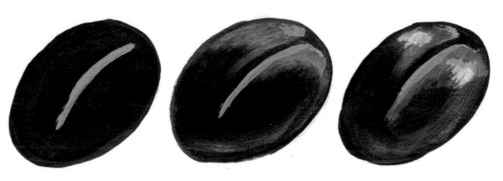

Turn an oval rock into a plum. Mix four parts Pansy Purple with one part Wrought Iron Black. Cover the entire surface. When dry, mix four parts Cloud White with one part Summer Sky Blue and add a touch of black paint to create a gray blue shade like the swatch above.

Use a liner brush to paint a slightly curved line lengthwise down the center of the rock like a cleft. Switch to a small stiff-bristled brush and pick up the same gray blue. Wipe away most of the paint then scrub on the remainder as shown.

Leave a narrow line of dark base coat showing along the upper side of the curving cleft. Also encircle the top or stem end with a rim of this soft blue. Smudge on a bit of white with a dry brush on either side of the cleft near the top. A small, light brown stem inside the top circle is optional.

Paint a Banana

Paint a Pear

1

Begin with a white base coat. When dry, fill in with Sunshine Yellow. Add a wide shadow of equal parts yellow and Pinecone Brown along the bottom.

2

Darken yellow/brown mix with touch of black and deepen lower half of shadow.

3

Mix Pinecone Brown and Black to get dark brown. Paint both ends and add a narrow center line.

4

Highlight the area above the narrow center line with a 1:1 mix of yellow and white.

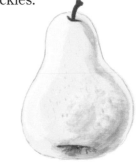

1

Base coat pear with white, let dry, then cover with Sunshine Yellow.

2

Mix equal parts Sunshine Yellow and Sprout Green. Shadow side and bottom. Add speckles.

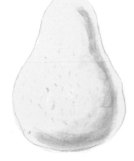

3

Add a touch of black to the green shadow mix and deepen the outside edges of the shadow. Also add more speckles.

4

Paint a dark brown stem and bottom end as shown. Highlight the left side with a yellow/white mix. Add a wash of Patio Brick to the center like a blush.

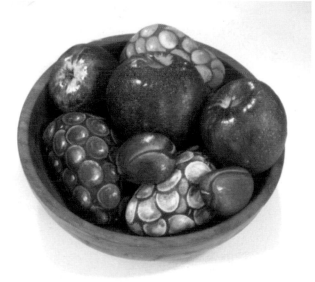

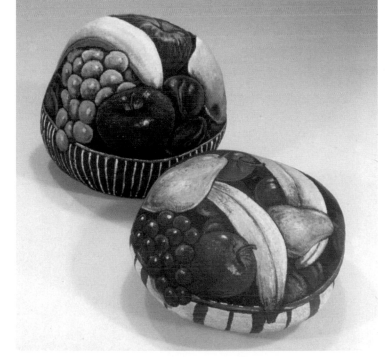

Display your rock fruit in a real bowl or paint a single large, round rock as a bowl of fruit

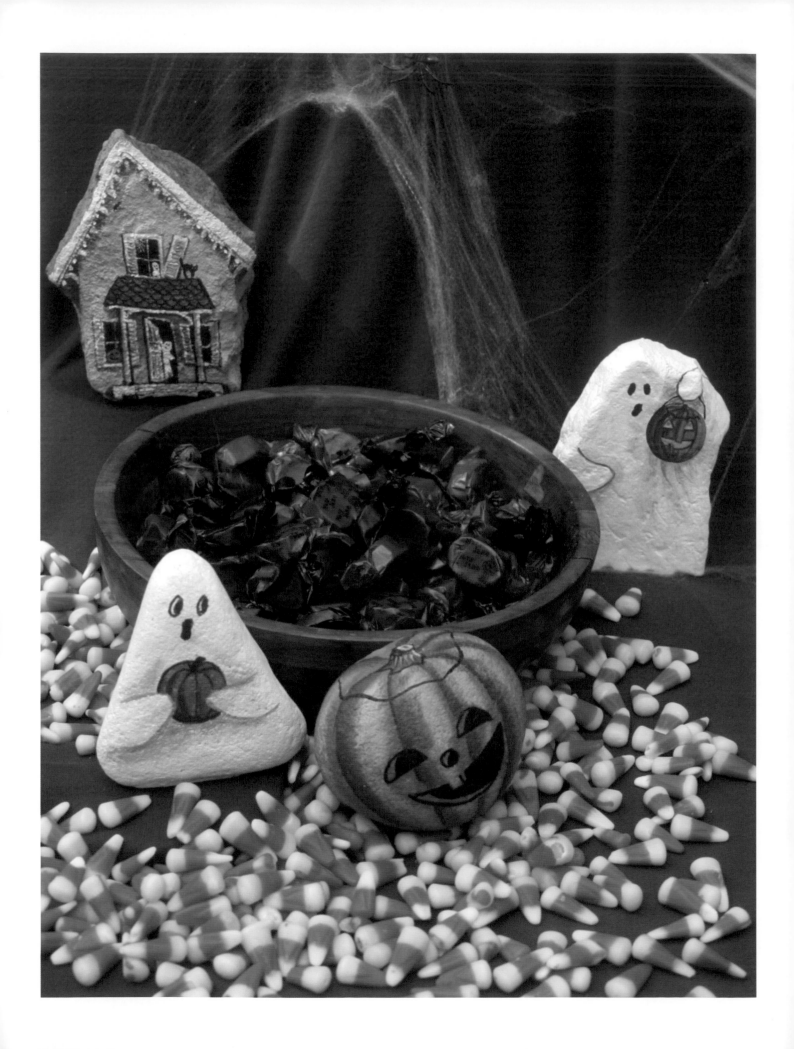

Spooky Stones

Paint these colorful Halloween decorations to haunt your home or office. Spooky rocks can guard your candy bowl or serve as a holiday centerpiece. Personalize them with names for place setting markers that double as party favors. Larger versions look 'spooktacular' on your doorstep or front porch!

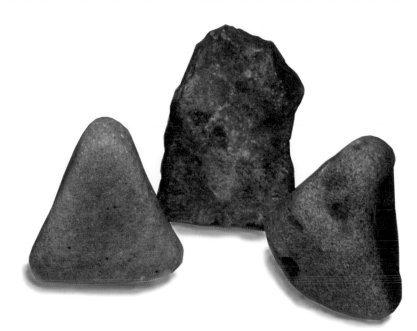

Choose Your Rock

Look for rocks that stand up on one flat end. The shapes may look like tombstones, rounded triangles or a more irregular shape, but for best results the rocks should be smooth and without jagged edges. Make sure your rock is clean and dry.

What you'll need for Ghosts:

- Pencil
- Assorted small and medium brushes including small flat and liner in size 0 or 1
- DecoArt Patio Paint (or equivalents) in:
  Cloud White
  Sunshine Yellow
  Petunia Purple or Blue Bell
  Tiger Lily Orange
  Geranium Red
  Wrought Iron Black

1 Apply Base Coat

Use a large, stiff brush to cover the entire rock except for the bottom with Cloud White paint. Darker rocks may require two coats.

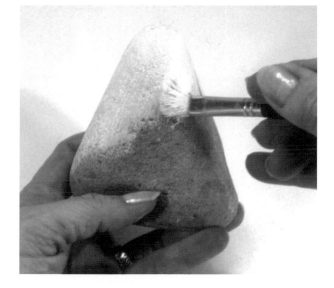

2 Draw on the Design

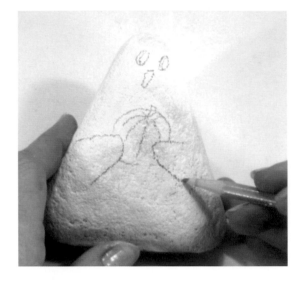

Begin by placing the round pumpkin shape in the center of the rock, slightly overlapped on either side by two oval shaped arms. Add two large oval eyes and a bigger irregular oval mouth.

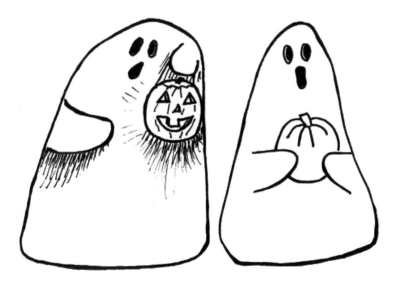

Modify the design as needed for your particular rock shapes

3 Undercoat Pumpkin and Add Shadows

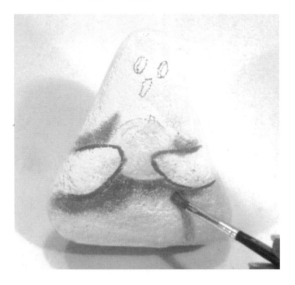

An undercoat of Sunshine Yellow will make the final coat 'pop'. Outline the shapes of the arms with Blue Bell (or Pansy Purple). Using the same color, switch to a small stiff brush and wipe away excess paint so that what remains can be scrubbed on to create shadows with a softly diffused look.

4 Paint the Pumpkin

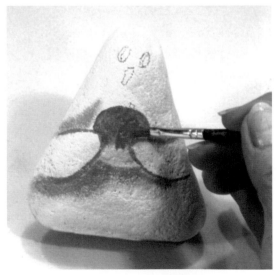

Rinse your brush and switch to Tiger Lily Orange to paint over the yellow base coat. Let dry.

52

5 Add Pumpkin Details

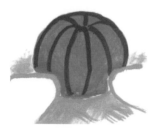 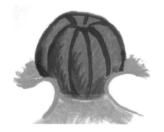 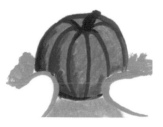

Use Geranium Red and a liner brush to outline top and ridge lines

Mix red with orange and apply with a small dry brush to shadow ridges as shown

Darken red with black to get a deep brown. Use a liner to outline along bottom, then add stem and darker lines to top

6 Finishing Touches

Use black paint and a liner brush to give your ghost two eyes and an open mouth. The eyes can be solid or you may outline the shapes and then add smaller ovals inside to make the ghost appear to be looking at something.

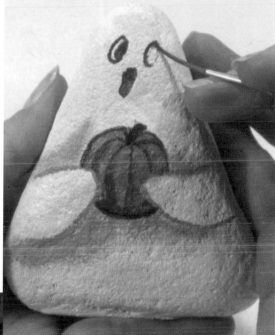

Windowsills, desktops, even bathroom counters could use a ghostly guest or two or three...

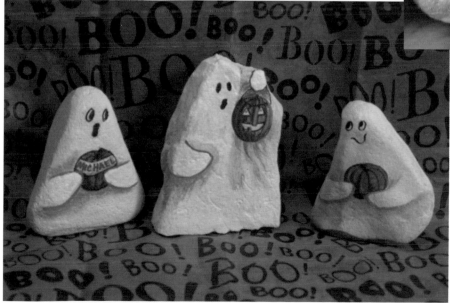

How to Paint

Rock O'Lanterns

It is hard not to grin back at these happy pumpkin faces. Rock O'Lanterns can be as small as pebbles or as big as an actual pumpkin. Decorate your home or office and make extras- everyone will want one. Unlike real pumpkins, your Halloween masterpieces will last forever!

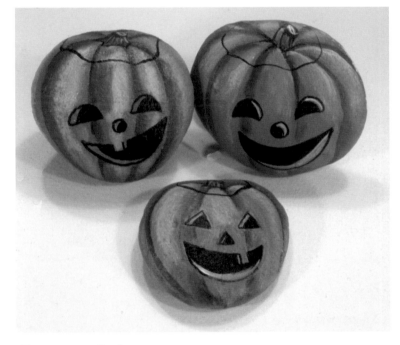

Choose your Rock

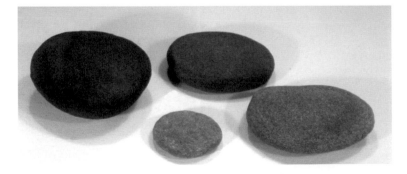

Flat rocks are more common than round ones and will work just fine as Rock O'Lanterns when propped against something or nestled into a candy dish. Tiny pebbles make great button covers when glued to store bought findings.

What you'll need for Pumpkins:

- Pencil
- Assorted small and medium brushes
- DecoArt Patio Paint (or equivalents) in:
  Sunshine Yellow
  Tiger Lily Orange
  Geranium Red
  Sprout Green
  Wrought Iron Black

1 Paint the Undercoat and Base Coat

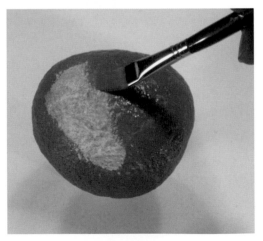

An undercoat of bright yellow will make the base coat of Tiger Lily Orange stand out. Use a stiff brush to apply each coat, and allow them to dry in between.

54

2 Draw the Features

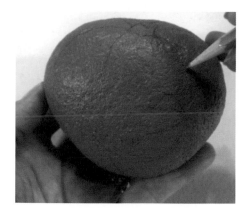

Use a pencil to sketch on the simple features. At the top draw a stem, then radiate lines to indicate the curved ridges that give pumpkins their distinctive contours.

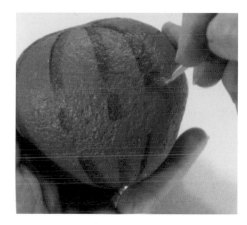

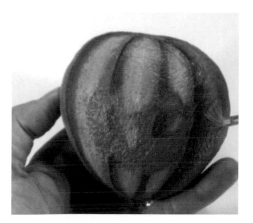

3 Darken Ridge Lines

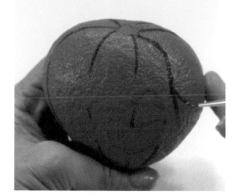

Establish the ridges by going over the guidelines with Geranium Red paint and a liner brush. Moisten the brush first so that the lines glide on smoothly.

4 Create Shadows

Use a larger, stiff-bristled brush and mix equal parts red and orange paint. Apply this mix in a wide swath along the right side of each darker line. Wipe your brush and use the dry bristles to blend and soften the edges of the swaths along the right side. Decorative painters may prefer to float the shadows on.

5 Add Highlights

Rinse your brush then mix equal parts of Sunshine Yellow and orange to get a paler orange shade. Use this to paint a swath along the left side of each of the dark red lines. Again use your dry brush to blend and soften the edges. Add a trace of white to the mix and blend it into the center of the light orange swath.

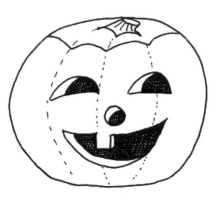

Use one of my designs or . . .

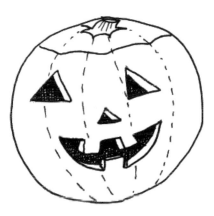

create one of your own!

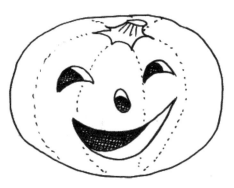

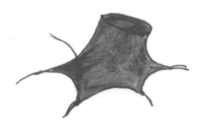 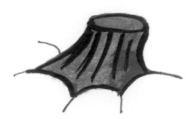 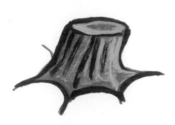

Fill in the stem shape with Sprout Green

Darken green with black then outline the stem shape and add ridges

Lighten green with yellow and highlight the top, side and a few nearby ridges

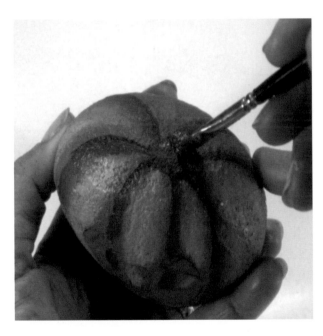

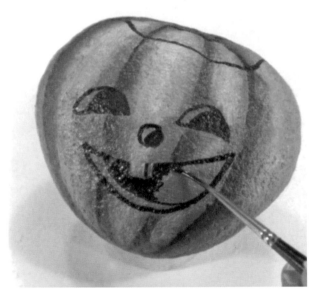

6 Paint the Stem

Use a small round or angular brush to fill in the stem shape with Sprout Green. For a realistic look, make sure that the bottom angles of the stem correspond to the contours of the pumpkin by matching them up with the dark red lines.

7 Outline and Fill in Features

Outline the features on your Rock O'Lantern using Wrought Iron Black and a moistened liner brush. Fill in the open areas with black, but leave narrow wedges uncovered along the inside edges of each feature to suggest the rind of the pumpkin. Add a line encircling the top where the lid would lift off. Outline around the edges of the stem and add a few narrow lines of texture to the sides as shown on stem illustration

8 Add Highlights to Stem

Mix enough yellow paint into a small amount of green to get a clearly lighter color. Use this to add highlights to the right hand edge of the stem and to create a circular top.

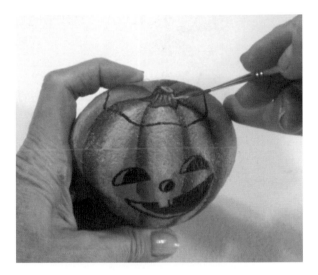

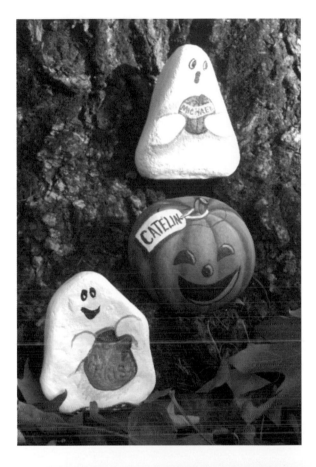

Tip: A coat of clear spray-on sealer like Krylon will protect the finished rock and brighten its colors

Paint personalized spooky rocks as party favors!

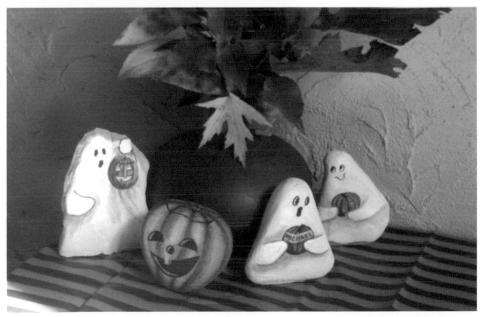

Add a bouquet of colored leaves to create a fun and attractive seasonal display

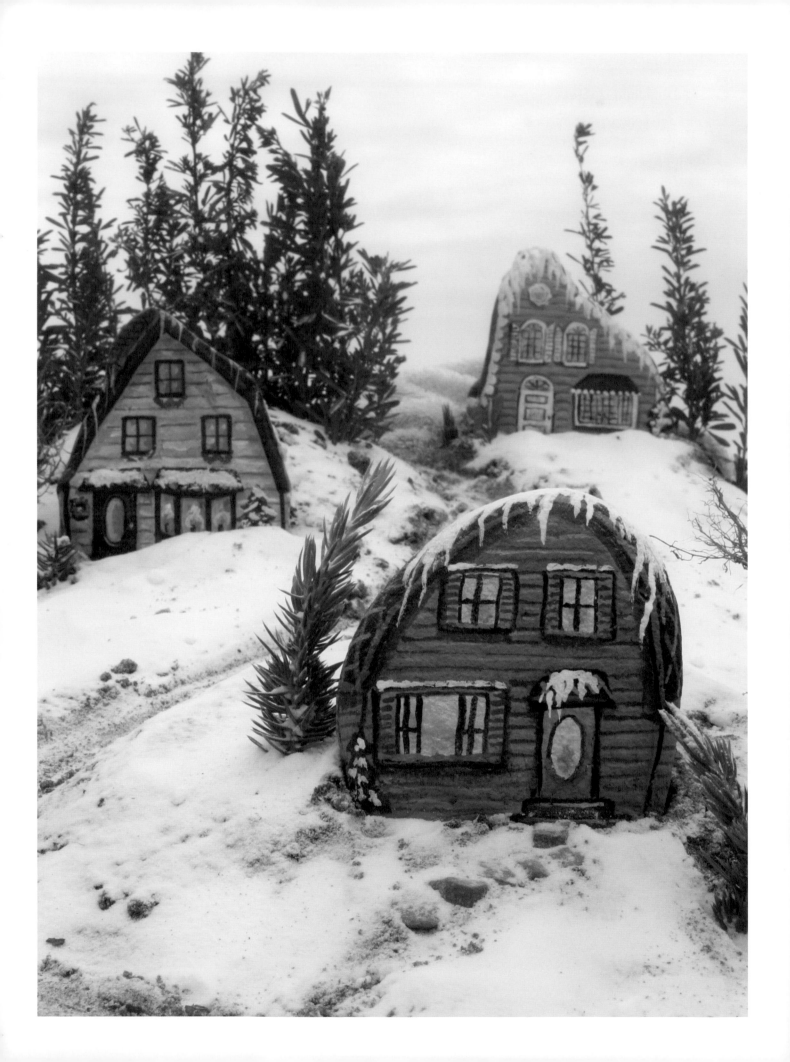

Holiday Houses

As a child I was intrigued by the little cardboard Christmas village my mother put out every year. While my memories of it survive, the houses themselves did not. If only they'd been made of rock! Rock houses and cottages are among the easiest projects for new painters. Paint a door and windows on almost anything and it begins to look like a house. Rocks with flat bottoms and angled or curving tops are surprisingly common and can often be found in backyards or along the roadside. Even broken pieces of brick or cement can be transformed into charming cottages. Make several versions in different colors and shapes to create your own heirloom snow village.

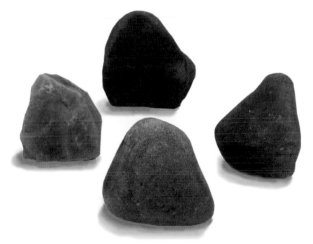

Choose your Rock or Rocks

House rocks should stand upright on a flat bottom with a top that resembles a peaked roof. The edges may be angular or rounded. If you are going to paint several cottages, look for rocks that seem to fit together as this group does.

Tip: When creating a group of houses, make all the doors the same height to establish scale

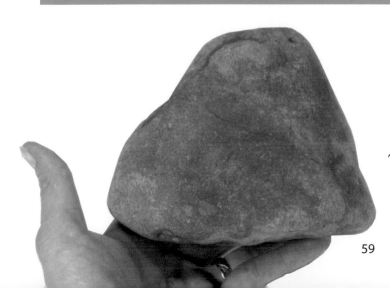

What you'll need:

- Pencil
- Straight edge ruler
- Assorted brushes including small and medium shaders, small round brushes and a liner in 0 or 1, optional- Deco Art Snow Writer or white dimensional paint
- DecoArt Patio Paint (or equivalents) in:
  Cloud White
  Dark Eucalyptus Green
  Sunshine Yellow
  Tango Blue
  Wrought Iron Black
  Patio Brick
  Summer Sky Blue
  Pine Green
  Geranium Red

The top of this rock doesn't come to a point, but it still suggests a roof-line. Make sure the rock is scrubbed clean and allowed to dry.

1 Draw on Design

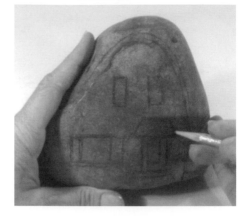

Use a regular pencil to draw a rectangular door, along side a window whose top is level with the door. Add one or two windows to the upper level, depending on the amount of room available on your rock. A porch roof over the door and shutters at the sides of the windows are nice touches. Use a small ruler to keep edges straight if needed.

2 Undercoat the Rock

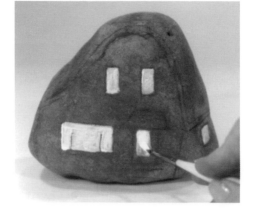

An undercoat of white paint makes subsequent window colors look more vibrant. Apply Cloud White with a small or medium shader or round brush. Let dry.

3 Paint the Walls

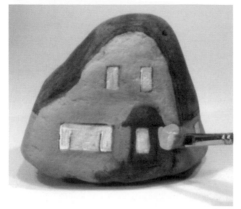

The color for the walls is a soft pastel made by mixing Dark Eucalyptus Green with an equal amount of Cloud White. Or combine Sprout Green with White and a smaller amount of Summer Sky Blue. Use a small or medium shader to paint the front, sides and the back. Add a door and other details to the back or leave it a solid color.

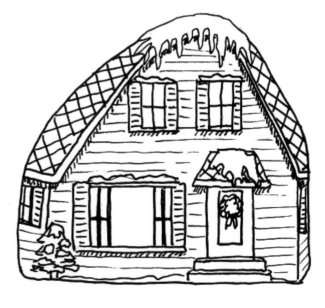

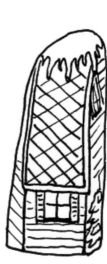

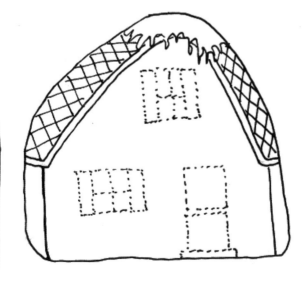

Pattern for front, sides and back of Holiday House. Door and windows on back are optional

4 Make Shadows and Outlines

Darken the remaining wall color with increments of black until it is noticeably darker. Use a small shader brush to paint a narrow edge of shadow below the roof line all the way around. Add shadows under each of the windows and below the porch roof. Switch to a liner brush and moisten the paint so that it glides smoothly to outline around the windows and door. Also use lines to establish the corners of your building beginning just inside the corners of the eaves. If you have a steady hand, give your cottage lapboard siding, or leave the walls plain as if covered with stucco. A line of lighter green over each board line will add to the illusion of dimension.

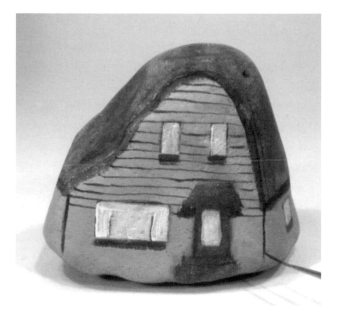

5 Fill in the Windows

Use Sunshine Yellow to fill in all windows, including the glass insert in the front door. A small shader works well for tight spaces. Next pick up just a trace of Patio Brick without rinsing your brush, blending the two to get a soft orange. Wipe away any excess paint then gently scrub this color into the lower halves of all the windows to add an inviting amber glow.

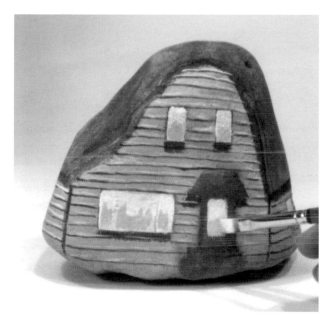

6 Paint the Roof

Choose a dark color like Tango Blue or another deep shade. A large shader can quickly fill in the roof up to the edge of the shadowed walls. Paint the porch roof the same way.

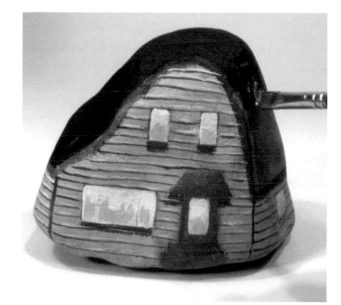

7 Add Zippy Trim

Colorful trim is a perfect way to add a festive look to your cottage. Use Summer Sky Blue and a small round brush to paint the eaves, leaving a narrow edge of the roof color in place between it and the shadows below. Lighten the blue paint with white to make a more pastel shade and use it to add a rectangular shutter to either side of every window. Also paint the edges of the door around the glass center.

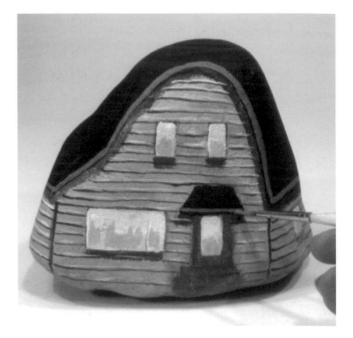

8 Choose a Shingle Pattern

For my roof I chose a criss-cross design, but there are many other options. Here are just a few:

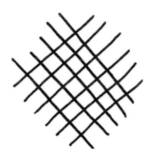

Diagonal cross-hatching

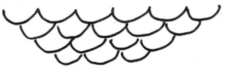

Layers of U-shaped loops

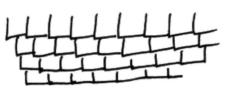

Layers of L-shaped angles

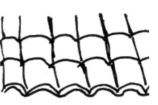

Barrel Tile

9 Detail the Roof

Apply the shingle pattern of your choice, using the same color used for the eaves. Loosening the paint with a bit of water will help your lines to go on smoothly. Hold the brush at a right angle to the surface for more control. Add shingles to the porch roof as well.

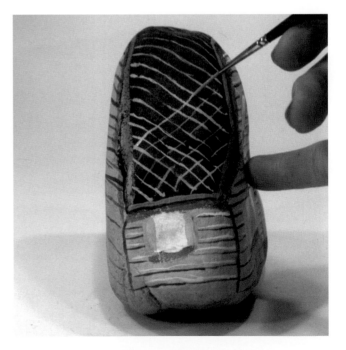

10 Add Defining Details

Rinse your liner brush and use Summer Sky Blue to add small horizontal louver lines to the shutters, then use black paint to lightly outline the outside edges of the windows, shutters and door. Add pane lines to the windows.

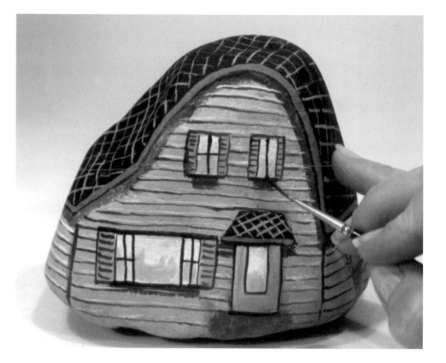

11 Paint the Steps

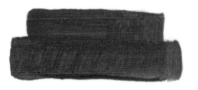

Choose a base color like Patio Brick or Pinecone Brown to fill in the shape of the steps

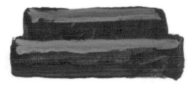

Lighten a bit of the base color with enough white to highlight the top of each step.

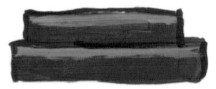

Darken another bit of base color with black and outline all edges to help them stand out.

12 Add Greenery

You can stop there and have a finished piece, or add more festive touches. Use a small round brush and Pine green to paint three telescoping triangles that form a small evergreen tree. Add a small wreath to the door with the same color.

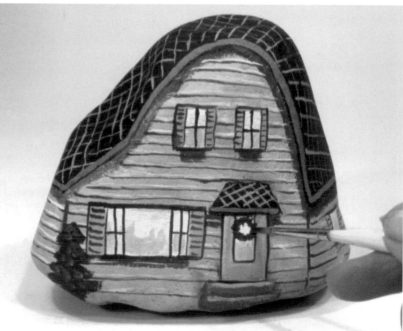

13 Let it Snow!

Apply white paint along the bottom edge of the rock to create the look of a snow drift. Use a medium shader to add narrow ledges of snow to the tops of all the windows. Paint snow on the porch roof and along the peak of the main roof, then use the edge of the brush to pull down narrow lines like icicles hanging over the eaves. Give the evergreen small clumps of snow along its branches. DecoArt's Snow Writer or white fabric paint will add a dimensional effect to these snowy additions and the narrow tip of their squeeze bottles makes them easy to use.

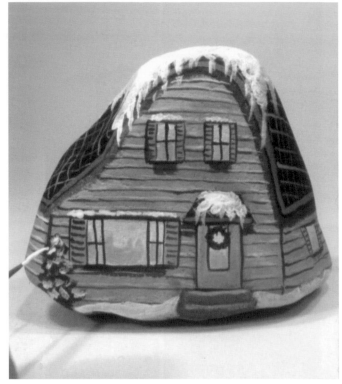

14 Finishing Touches

Use Geranium Red and a liner brush to give the wreath a stylized bow. Other options include adding green garlands that drape in graceful loops below the windows. Decorate the outside tree with tiny balls of color applied with the tip of your brush handle. You might even paint a decorated tree showing in the front window.

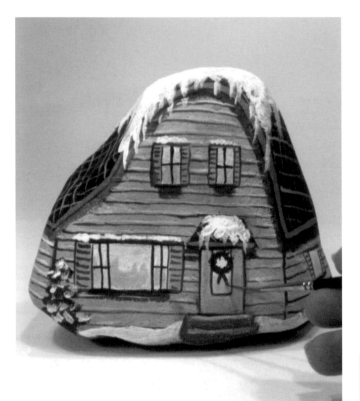

Start a family tradition by building your own snow village. The trees are bits of driveway gravel painted deep green then covered with dabs of white paint

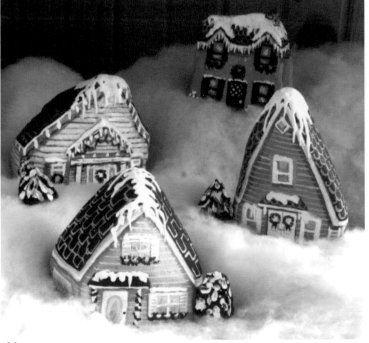

More Ideas...

I used Sno-Tex on this house to give the snow more dimension. Add sparkle to the tree with glitter glue or metallic paint garlands

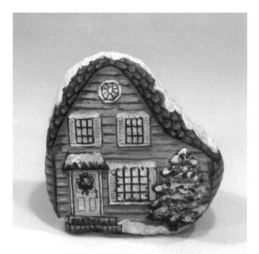

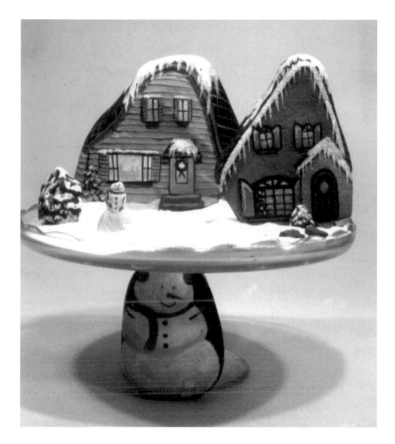

A pedestal cake stand serves as the base for this holiday centerpiece and Borax, the laundry additive, provides snowy drifts. The smaller snowman was made by gluing pebbles together. I painted a single rock snowman to dress up the pedestal. The free-standing evergreens are more painted rocks

Halloween Houses are another fun project you may want to try. Paint windows black to show off ghostly inhabitants. You can also add cats, bats, pumpkins, spooky trees and even spider's webs

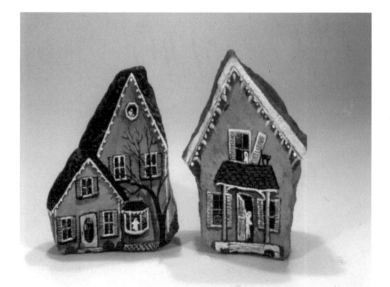

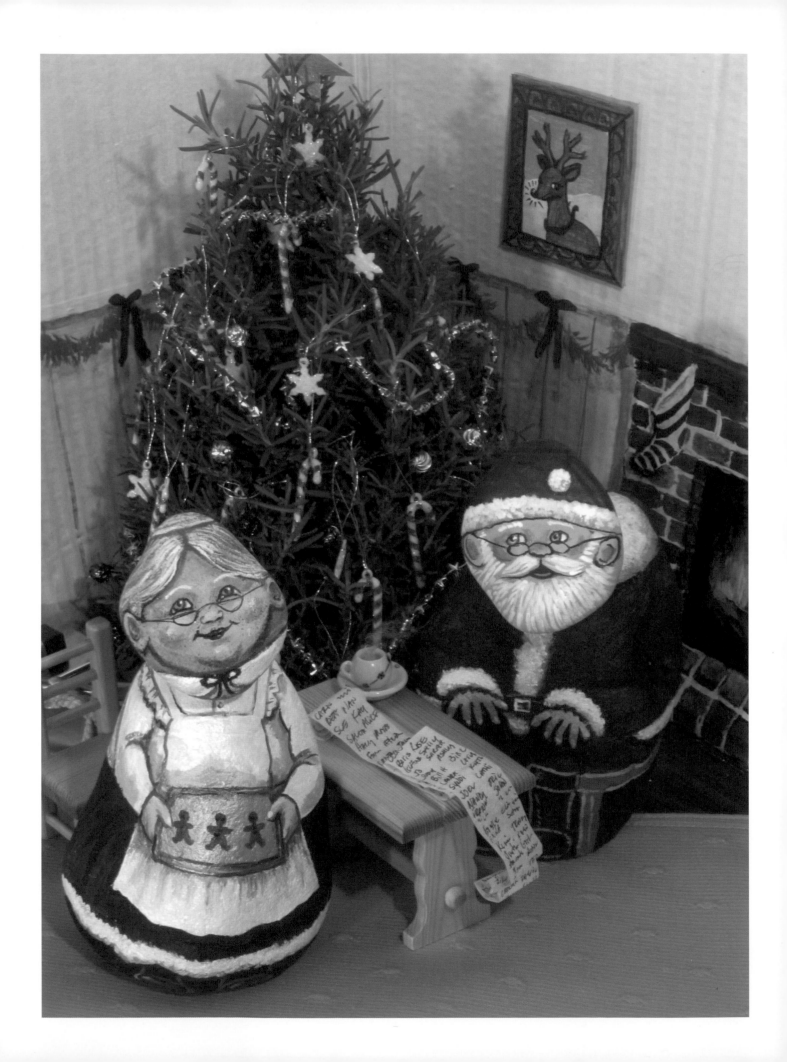

Rockin' Santa

If you are a Santa fan, painted rocks are a splendid way to celebrate that 'right jolly old elf'! Smiling Santa faces can be used to dress up a special gift or as tree ornaments. Tiny Santa faces make cute holiday jewelry or button covers. Paint extras as festive little tokens to hand out all through the season. Attach faces to larger rocks to create adorable Santa Claus figures suitable for display indoors or out.

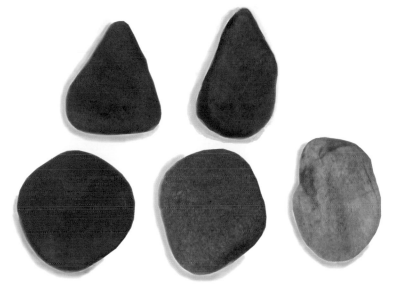

What you'll need:

- Pencil
- Assorted brushes including small and medium flats or shaders, small round brushes and a liner in 0 or 1
- DecoArt Patio Paint (or equivalents) in:
  Sunshine Yellow
  Wrought Iron Black
  Cloud White
  Larkspur Blue
  Summer Sky Blue
  Geranium Red
  Pinecone Brown
- Heavy duty glue like Liquid Nails or E6000

Choose a Rock

Select a flat rock with rounded edges. With imagination, almost any shape can be turned into a Santa face. A pointed end can be the peak of his hat or an angular beard.

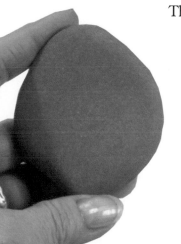

The rock I chose would be a perfect size to use alone as an ornament. Always wash your rock and let it dry before painting.

1 Draw on the Design

Try your hand at copying this simple design. Each Santa will look different because rock shapes vary. That is part of the fun!

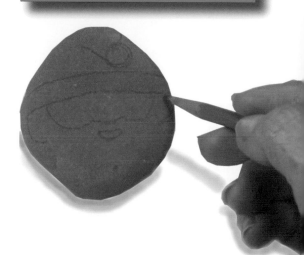

2 Paint Undercoat for Hat

Fill in the top of the cap (but not the brim or tassel) with yellow, using a small flat brush. Paint the cap on the back side of the rock as well.

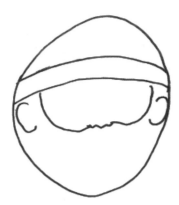

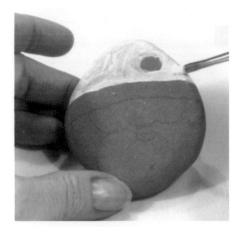

3 Paint the Face

Mix colors as shown to get skin tone. Paint with a clean round or flat brush. If the rock is very dark, a white base coat for the face and ears will improve coverage.

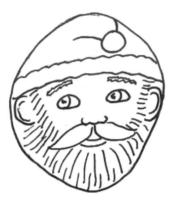

Pattern for Santa Face

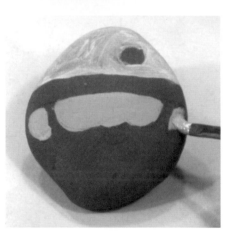

Face color recipe

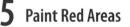

Mix 3 parts white with one part each of Sunflower Yellow and Geranium Red

4 Paint Brim and Beard Undercoats

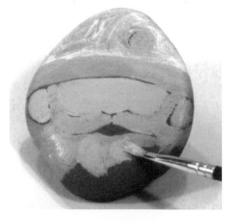

Larkspur Blue is a perfect background to set off the white fur brim and fluffy beard. Mix a similar color by adding white and a touch of black to medium blue.

5 Paint Red Areas

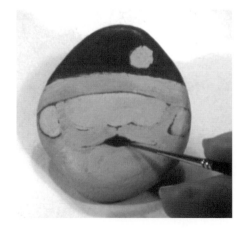

Use Geranium Red to cover the yellow base coat for the hat. Switch to a liner brush to give the mouth area a curving bottom lip.

6 Draw Facial Features

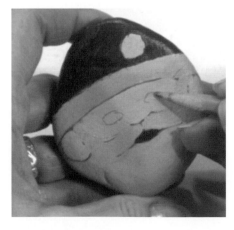

Draw two widely spaced eyes in the center of the face. Eye shapes may be oval, round or even cheery little crescents.

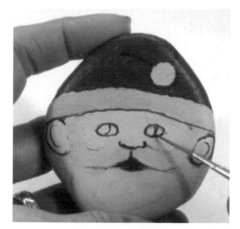

7 Add Defining Outlines

Mix deep maroon by adding a trace of black to red. Use a liner brush to outline all the parts of the hat and around all the facial features. Divide the mustache just below the nose and underline along its bottom edge on either side. Darken the upper portion of the mouth. Place iris circles to the same side on each eye as if glancing sideways.

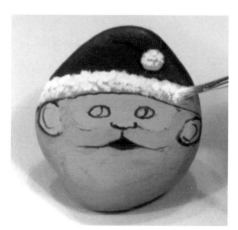

8 Daub on Fleecy Trim

A stiff or scruffy flat brush is best for daubing on fleecy texture. Allow some of the base coat to show, especially at the bottom edge of the tassel and along the lower half of the fur brim. Apply the white more solidly along the tops. Overlap the outlines here and there to enhance a fluffy look.

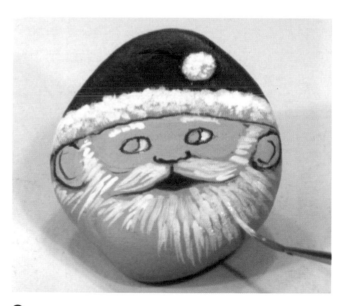

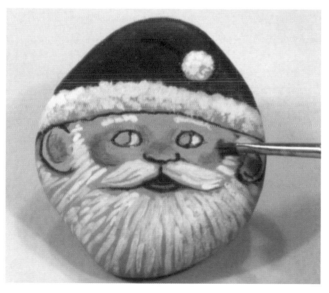

9 Paint White Details and Beard

Use the tip of a liner brush to fill in the whites of the eyes and to lightly dot on two narrow eyebrows. Fill in the mustache with angled strokes, leaving blue outlines to define its shape. Loosen the paint and fill in the beard with dense, overlapping rows of delicate strokes that allow some of the blue base coat to show through.

10 Contour with Soft Tints

Soften red slightly with a touch of white and use a liner brush to make a single narrow line along the top of the lip. Add enough water to turn the remainder into a transparent tint. Fill in the insides of both ears and add a soft blush to the outside edges of each cheek. Tint the top of nose above the tip and along the inside edge of each eye. Use a small dry brush to softly blend away any sharp edges.

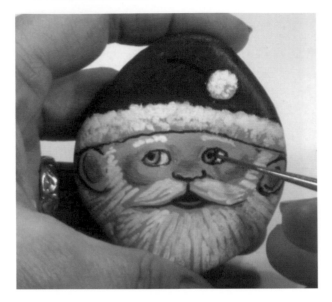

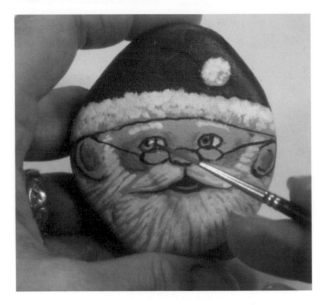

Fill in the eyes with Summer Sky Blue. Pick up a bit of white on the same liner brush without rinsing, and add a half circle of lighter blue along the bottom half of each iris, then place a single dot of black in the center of each one.

If you have a steady hand, you may also opt to add a pair of glasses perched low on the nose. A tiny dot of white in each eye will give Santa his merry twinkle!

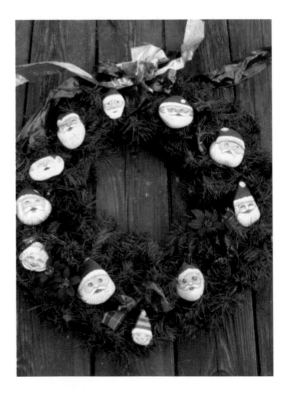

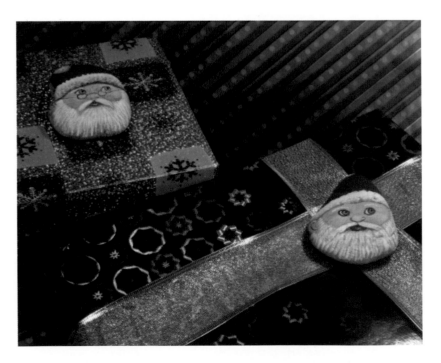

Dress up a wreath with weather-proof Santas. Painting them makes a wonderful holiday activity for the whole family.

Use smiling Santas to decorate those special gifts. A hot glue gun makes it easy!

Paint Santa's Body

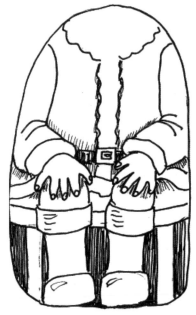

Front view

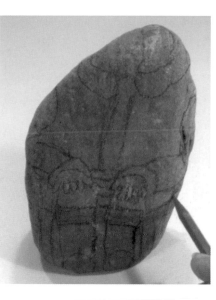

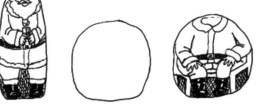

Tip: Use wood filler to build up an uneven bottom if needed

1 Draw on Design

Select an upright rock with a flat base. For proper proportion, the body should measure 2 to 3 times the height of the head. Once the rock is clean and dry, use a pencil to sketch on or trace and transfer the pattern elements. If you have a very tall rock, your Santa could be standing, but seated Santa rocks are more common.

2 Paint Undercoat

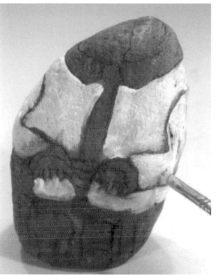

Yellow paint will make red clothes look brighter. Leave guidelines uncovered.

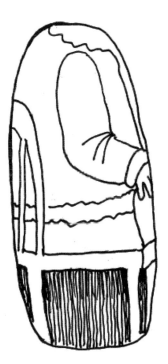

Side view

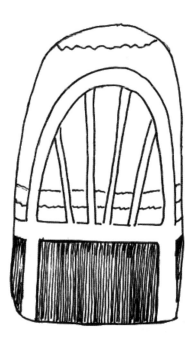

Back view

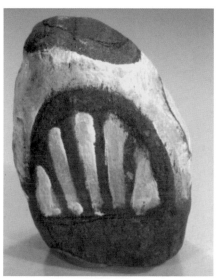

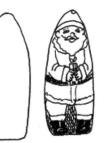

Tall rocks could fit standing figures. Round rocks make roly-poly Santas

3 Paint Blue Undercoat for Fleecy Trim

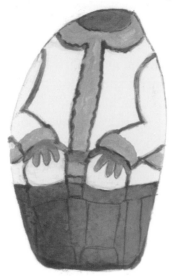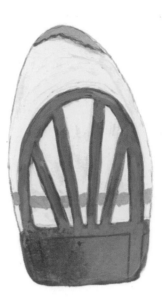

Use a small flat brush and Larkspur Blue to paint an undercoat for the fur trim on the coat. The trim below the belt goes around the rock.

4 Paint Fingers and Neck

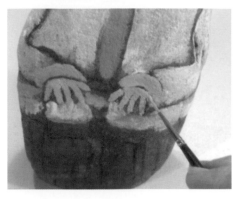

Combine the same colors used for the face to fill in the neck area inside the collar. Switch to a liner brush to paint the hands, splaying the fingers out over the knees.

5 Fill in Chair Parts

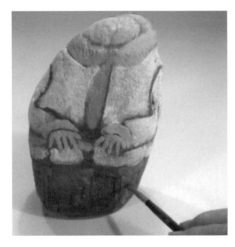

Switch to a small flat or round brush and Pinecone Brown to fill in the back, legs and seat of the chair, including the segments showing between Santa's knees and on the back side.

6 Fill in Boots and Define Contours

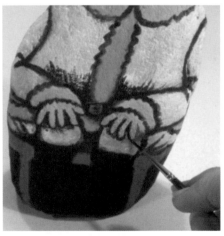

Use black paint to fill in the boots. Black paint also 'erases' areas like the spaces between the chair legs all the way around. Switch to a liner brush to outline around each element of Santa's body. Add creases to sleeves and pants. Outline the chair back and slats, then use a small flat brush to create the suggestion of shadows on Santa's midsection between and above his hands. Apply these with a dry brush for a softer look.

7 Color in Santa's Suit

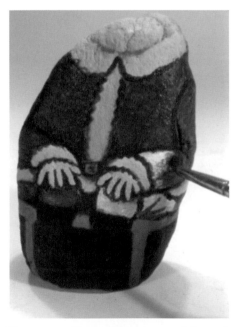

Use a medium flat or round brush and red paint to fill in Santa's suit, covering all the areas previously base coated yellow. Paint right over the black outlines and shadows with a light coat of red to soften them. Let dry.

8 Daub on Fleecy Trim

Use white paint and a scruffy flat brush to daub white paint onto the collar, cuffs and the trim of the jacket as you did earlier on the brim of Santa's hat. Allow some of the blue undercoat to show through, especially along the lower edges to suggest the look of shadows.

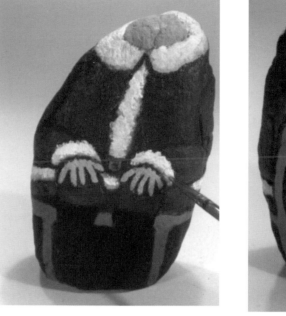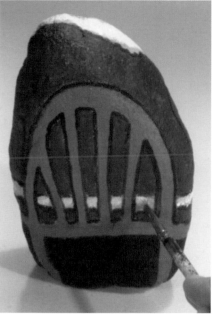

9 Detail Fingernails and Boots

Switch to a liner brush and use white paint to add small round fingernails to the ends of Santa's fingers. Rinse the brush. Add just enough black paint to a drop of Larkspur Blue to create a light blue-gray. Outline the edges of the black boots with this color to help them stand out. Paint folded-down cuffs at the tops of the boots and rounded toes at the bottoms. For more depth, create soft sheens of this gray in sets of short horizontal strokes on the boot cuffs and down along the same side on both boots. Paint a small crescent of sheen on the same side of each curving boot toe. At Santa's waist, add two narrow parallel lines to suggest the top and bottom edge of a belt.

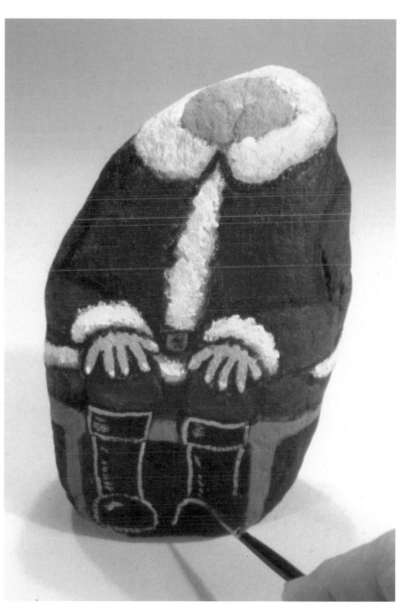

73

10 Paint the Buckle

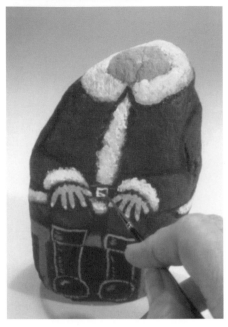

Use Sunshine Yellow to add a small square buckle in the center of the belt lines.

11 Highlight the Chair Front and Back

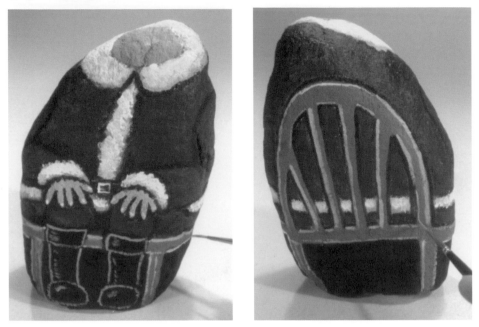

Lighten Pinecone Brown with enough white paint to get a lighter brown color and use it to outline the tops, bottoms and sides of the chair elements.

12 Join Santa's Head and Body

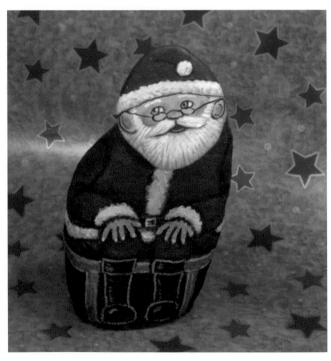

Use a heavy duty glue like Liquid Nails or E 2000 to secure Santa's head to his body. You may need to prop up or support the head rock to insure it sets up properly.

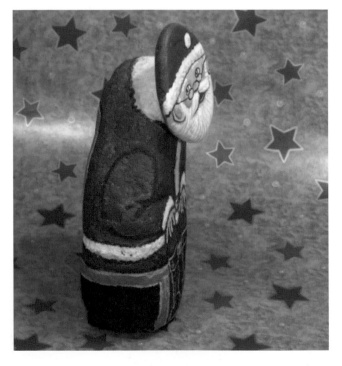

The addition of the head will make Santa appear to be leaning forward in his chair as if eager to hear the next holiday wish. Tipping or tilting the head is another way to add personality.

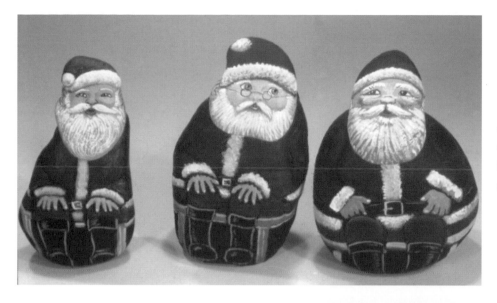

Because every rock is different, each rock body and head combination will be a unique creation, even when painted the same way

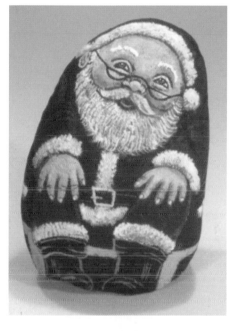

Tip- When painting a very round rock like the one to the right, keep the chair legs straight rather than allowing them to follow the curved contours of the rock

Santa may also be painted on a single rock if you find one that allows sufficient room for the head

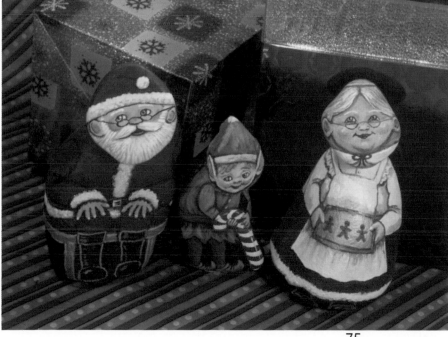

Display your holiday figures as a group. Don't be surprised if you find yourself needing to paint extra sets for friends and family!

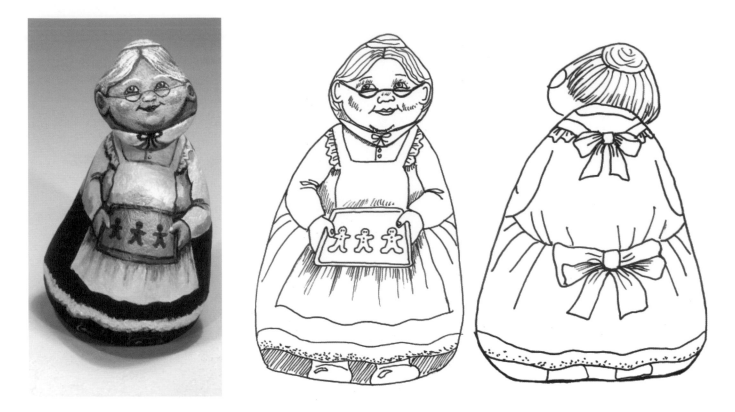

Mrs. Claus is fun and easy to paint, too. Use gray to shadow her blouse and apron. Her baking pan is metallic silver and the cookies are painted with Pinecone Brown

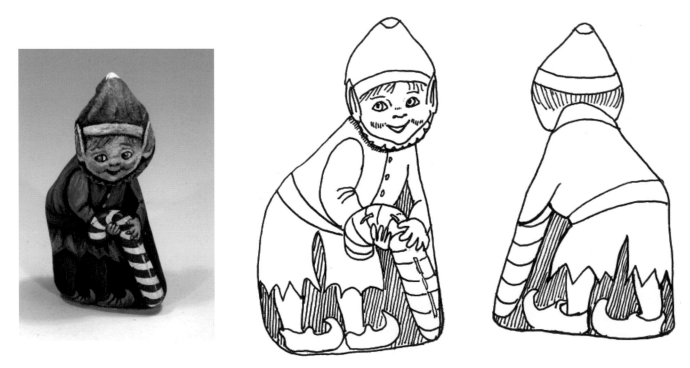

This is just one way to fit a Christmas Elf on a rock. I used a candy cane to fill in the extra space on the side. Use dark paint to 'erase' the areas around and between the legs. Old fashioned toys or festively wrapped packages also make cute props

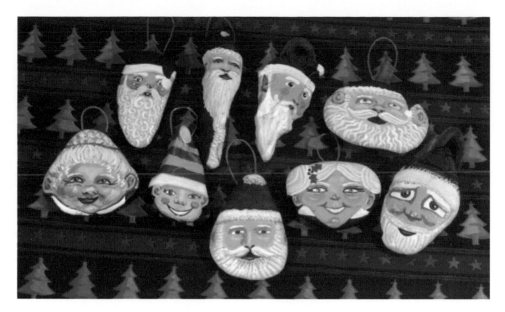

My daughter Kira and her friend Kevin helped paint these ornaments. Smaller faces make cute button covers and jewelry

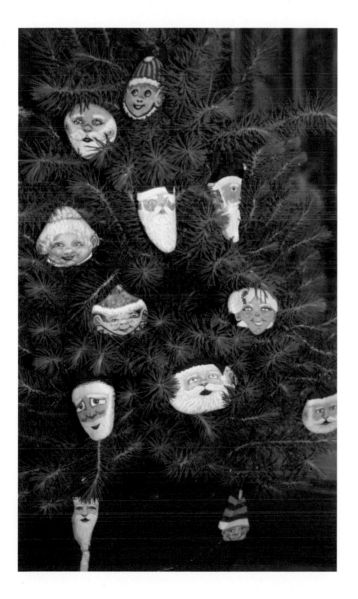

Rockin' Santa, Mrs. Claus and Elf ornaments really dress up a tree and are just about impossible to break! Use them alone or mix them in with your other decorations. Pipe cleaners, ribbon or wire hangers are attached to the backs with Liquid Nails

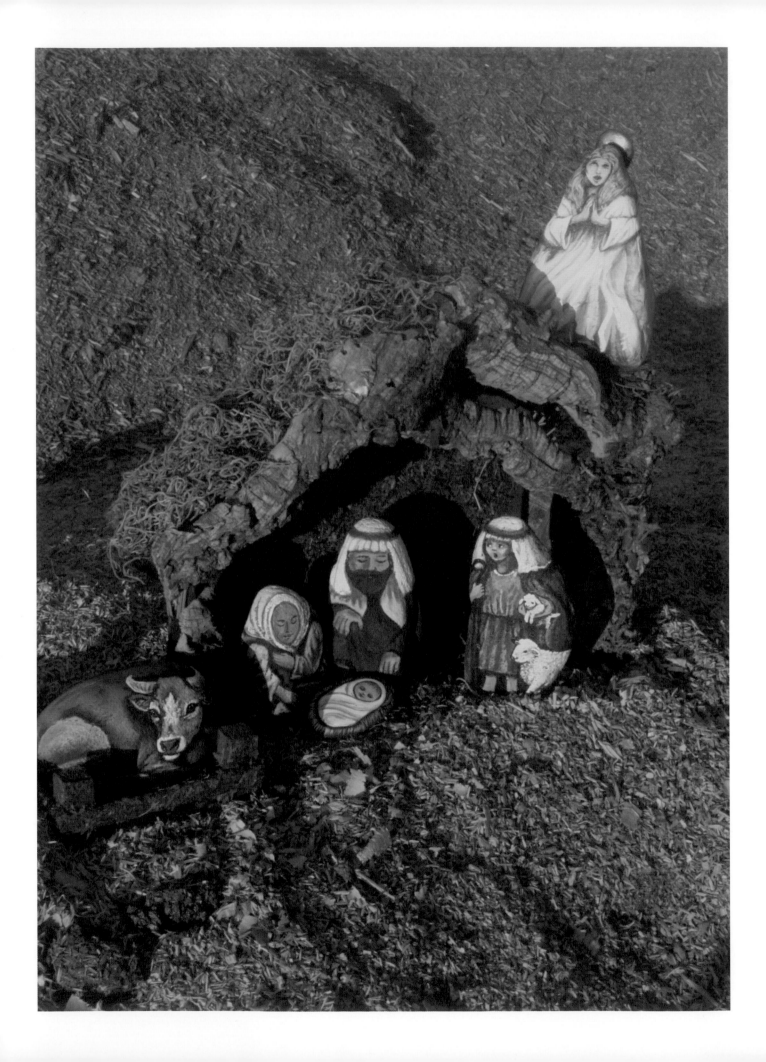

Nativity Scene

Imagine creating your own one-of-a-kind Nativity set, each lovingly-crafted figure perhaps destined to be treasured by future generations of your family. The infant is a perfect place to start and also makes a wonderful holiday craft project for children. Painting a bed of straw and swaddling clothes helps illustrate those sometimes confusing terms in a way kids can understand. The adult figures are a bit more complex, but they are still simple enough for beginning artists. Experienced painters may enjoy adding more elaborate or classical details to their figures.

Paint the Baby

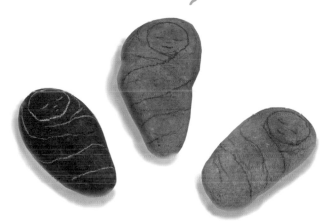

Select a Rock

Almost any small, smooth oval stone may be used to create an infant. It's a good idea to match up the other pieces at the same time if you plan to paint a complete nativity scene so that all the figures will be in proper proportion. Make sure the rock is clean and dry.

What you'll need for the Baby:
- Pencil
- Assorted brushes including small and medium shaders long or short liners and a small, stiff bristled brush
- DecoArt Patio paints (or equivalents) in:
  Pine Cone Brown
  Patio Brick
  Wrought Iron Black
  Blue Bell or Larkspur Blue
  Cloud White
  Sunshine Yellow or Sunflower Yellow
  Pot O' Gold

Larger rocks like this one are easier to paint than smaller ones, especially for young children

1 Draw on the Design

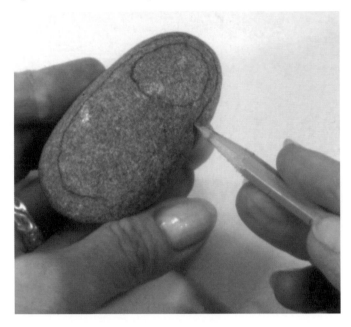

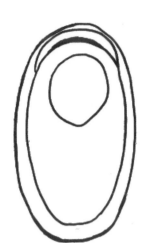 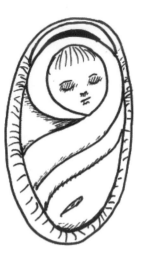

Basic pattern shapes   *Pattern with details*

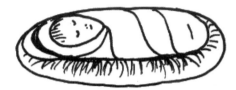

Side view

Make a small circle for the head at one end of the rock. Then draw an oval that is slightly smaller than the outside edges of the rock and encircles the head as shown.

2 Paint Undercoat for the Hay

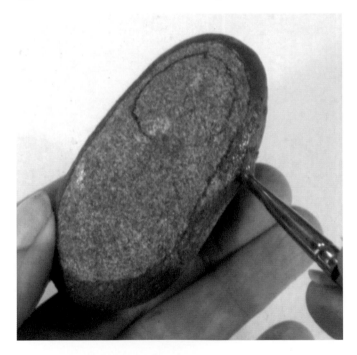

Use a small shader brush and Pine Cone Brown to paint the entire area outside the oval. Paint around the lower edges of the stone so that no plain surface shows. Patio Brick may be used as a substitute.

3 Add Shadows and Texture

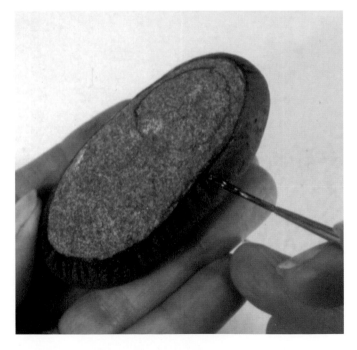

Use a long or short liner brush and black paint to encircle the oval shape, then stroke on tiny lines that radiate out all the way around the oval. This suggests the rough texture of the straw and also helps make the baby's shape stand out.

4 Paint the Swaddling Base Coat

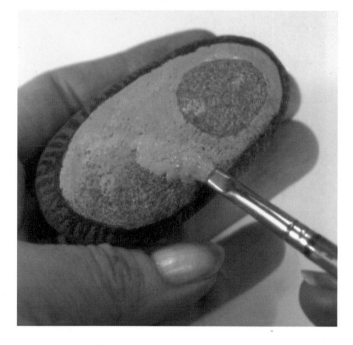

A rich color like Blue Bell will set off the white swaddling and also provides natural looking shadows and folds when narrow curves are left uncovered. Use a small or medium sized shader brush to fill in the body oval.

5 Undercoat for Head and Halo

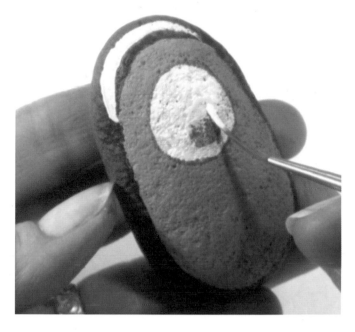

Use white paint and a small brush to make a crescent shaped halo above the head. Also fill in the head with white, and give it a slightly pointed chin.

6 Paint Swaddling with Dry Brush

For the soft look of cloth, use a small, stiff brush to pick up white paint, then wipe away most of the pigment so that what remains must be scrubbed on. Encircle the head as shown, leaving a narrow edge of base coat uncovered on either side. Bring that swath down so that it wraps around the baby's chest to end on the other side of the body. Add several other curving strips of varying widths below, each one defined by edges of base coat. I left a small line showing along the center of the bottom swath to suggest a crease. Lightly fill in the center of the small angle between the swaddling strips at the baby's shoulder.

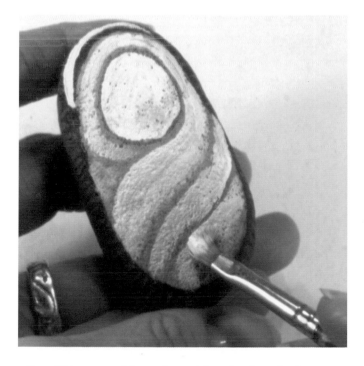

Scrubbing on white paint with a dry brush gives a soft texture to the swaddling clothes.

7 Paint the Manger Hay

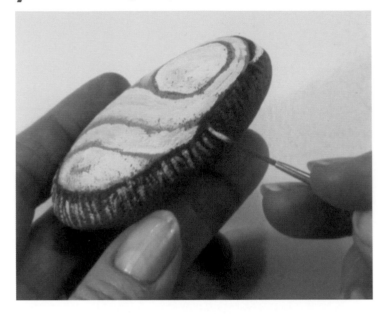

Use a liner or other delicate brush and Sunflower or Sunshine Yellow paint to create a fringe of strokes that start just beyond the dark outline of the baby and radiate outward along the edges all the way around the rock.

Color Recipes for Painting Skin Tones

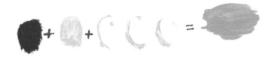

Recipe for flesh color paint using Geranium Red, Sunflower Yellow and Cloud White

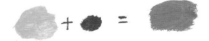

Recipe for face shadows created by darkening flesh color with Patio Brick

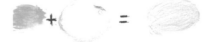

Recipe for face highlighting made by adding flesh color to a larger amount of Cloud White

8 Fill in the Face Shape

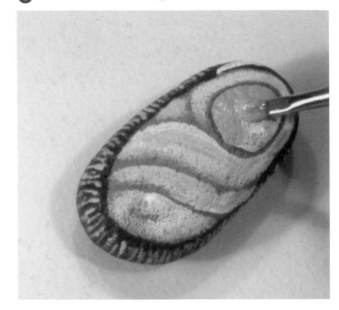

Combine the colors shown for the skin tone recipe. Use a small brush to fill in the entire face circle, but leave the dark outline surrounding it in place for definition.

9 Create Face Shadows

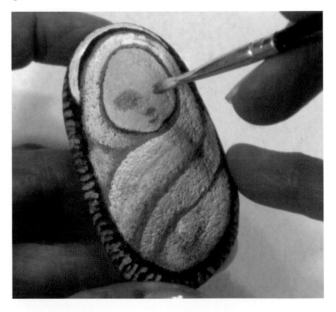

Add small increments of Patio Brick to flesh tone until you have a clearly darker shade. Choose a small, stiff brush to apply shadows to the face, starting with two small, widely spaced ovals at the midline of the face. Add a tiny smudge for the nose shadow and another below that as a shadow beneath the mouth. Remove most of the pigment from your brush before rubbing a curve of soft blush along the outside of each cheek.

10 Add Highlights to Face

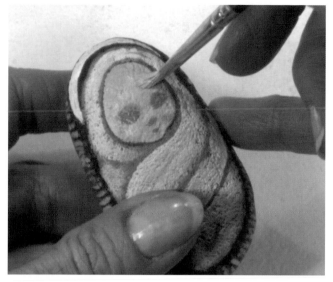

Rinse your brush and give the face soft highlights using lightened flesh tone. Apply with a dry brush so that the paint must be scrubbed on. Lighten the center portion of the forehead, the bridge of the nose and a narrow area directly below each of the two oval eye shadows.

11 Paint the Features

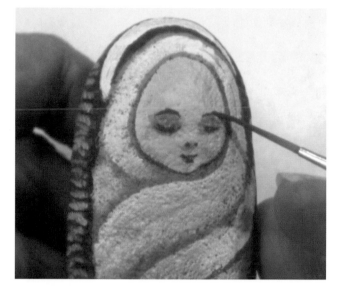

Switch to a liner brush and use Patio Brick, darkened with a touch of black, to create small crescent eye shapes at the lower edge of each eye shadow and eyebrows at the top. Lightly dot on two tiny nostrils just above the nose shadow. Give the baby a small curving upper lip and a smaller lower lip.

12 Paint and Highlight the Hair

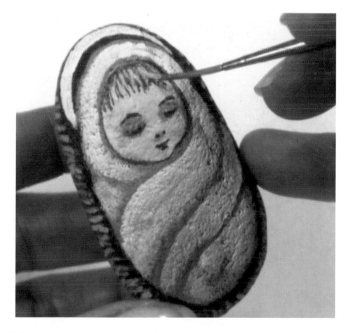

Use the same darkened Patio Brick to create a fringe of hair along the top of the head, then rinse and switch to Sunflower or Sunshine Yellow. Stroke a set of lighter hair lines on top of the darker set.

13 Fill in the Halo

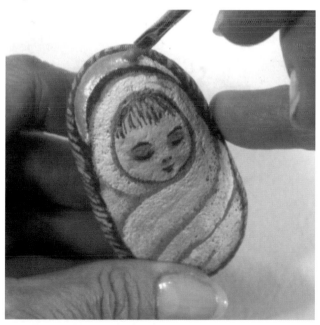

Fill in the narrow half circle of the halo with a metallic paint like Pot O' Gold. These tiny bundled babes make lovely little gifts around the holidays or could become the centerpiece of your hand painted creche.

Paint Mary and Joseph

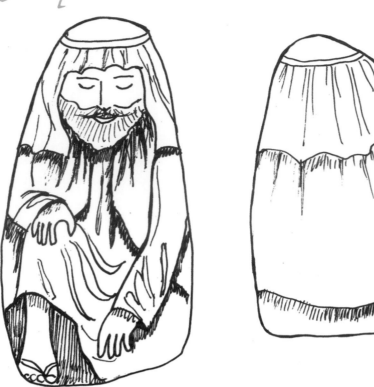

Design for Joseph- front and back

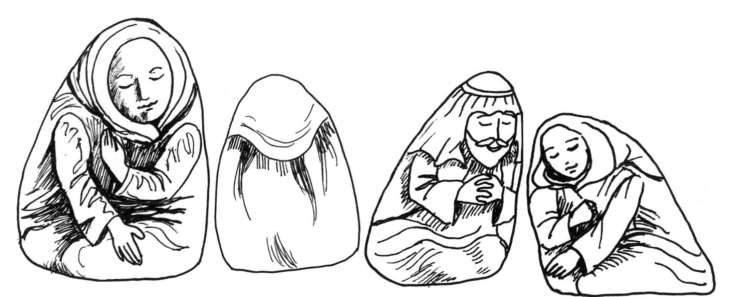

Design for Mary- front and back   *Alternate design for figures*

Select Your Figure Rocks

Many shapes will work, but an important consideration in choosing rocks for the figures is keeping them in proportion to one another and to the baby. Generally, I prefer Mary seated with both legs tucked or folded beneath her body.

Joseph is taller as if raised up on one or both knees. Look for a more upright rock with a flat base for Joseph and a shorter, more rounded rock for Mary. Once chosen, scrub the rocks well and allow them to dry.

84

1 Draw on Designs for Mary

Each rock shape will be slightly different so make adjustments in the placement of the hands or the angles of the heads as needed.

Mary has one hand stretching downward as if reaching out to her child. Use a white charcoal or regular pencil to draw on the basic elements, beginning with oval head shapes, the arms and hands. If you are not happy with your initial attempt at laying out the pattern, wash the lines away and start again.

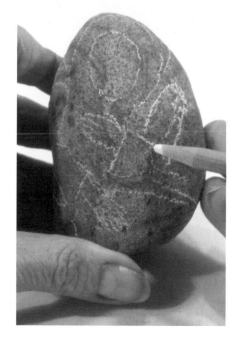

What you'll need for

Joseph

- White charcoal pencil
- Assorted brushes
- DecoArt Patio Paint (or equivalents) in:
  Wrought Iron Black
  Patio Brick
  Cloud White
  Sunflower Yellow
  Geranium Red
  Patio Brick
  Summer Sky Blue

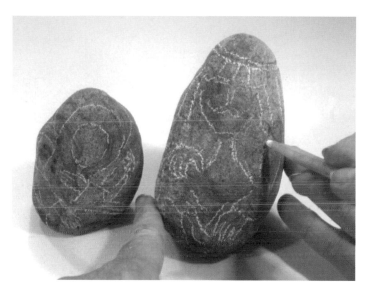

And for Joseph

Place Joseph's head first, then add his headdress, arms, hands and one foot if he is kneeling upon one knee. Draw on his layered tunic last.

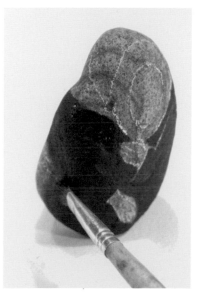

2 Paint the Robes

Fill in Mary's robes with Tango Blue or mix a deep blue by adding increments of black to bright blue until you reach a color between navy and royal blue. Use a size 4 or 6 shader brush. Leave the hands unpainted.

For Joseph's robe, add Wrought Iron Black to a small puddle of Patio Brick until you get a deep chocolate brown color. Use a 4 or 6 shader to fill in the robe, leaving the tunic and hands unpainted.

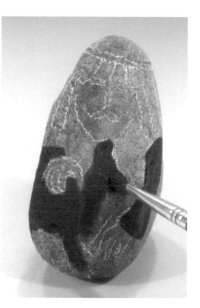

85

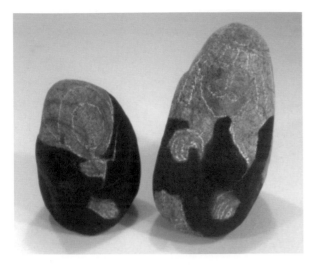

Once their robes are filled in the designs should be easier to see and adjust if necessary

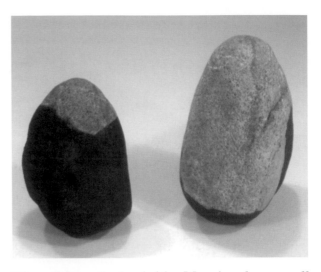

Viewed from the backside, Mary's robe goes all the way around while only the hem below Joseph's tunic will show

3 Paint the Head Wear

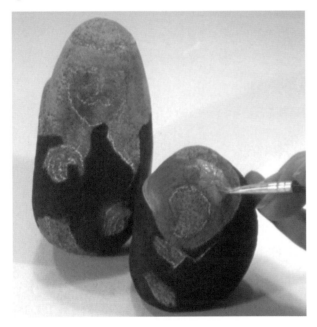

For head coverings on both figures, mix 4 parts of white with 1 part black to get a deep shade of gray. Use a small shader brush to fill in Mary's scarf right up to the edges of the face oval. Joseph's headdress is short across his forehead and longer on both sides as well as in back. You can leave a narrow strip around his crown unpainted where the headband encircles it, or cover the whole headdress and add the band later.

4 Paint Face and Hands

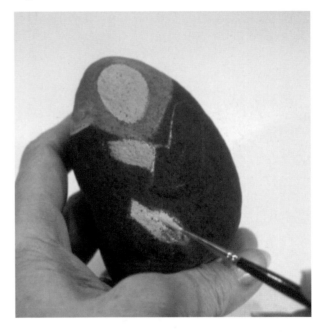

Combine equal amounts of Sunflower Yellow and Cloud White, then add increments of Geranium Red until you reach a flesh tone similar to the swatch provided for the infant. Use it and a small flat or round brush to fill in Mary's oval face. Use the same brush to begin Mary's hands, but switch to a liner brush to add her delicate fingers.

5 Highlight the Scarf

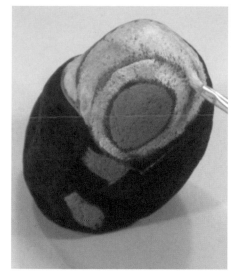

Use white paint and a small flat brush to encircle the head, leaving curving gray lines uncovered as folds. Leave an edge of gray in place to define the face shape. Below the chin have one narrow end overlap the other as if tucked into the top of the robe.

6 Highlight the Robe

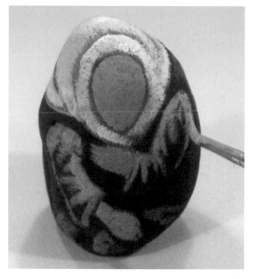

Add enough white paint to the blue robe color to get a more pastel shade. Use a small flat or shader brush to create highlights and suggest creases and gathers along the tops of Mary's sleeves and along the rounded shapes of her shoulders. Define the lower edges of the sleeves with thinner lines. Use the pattern provided for guidance in placing the highlights where they should go. Suggest the shape of folded legs by stroking nearly horizontal highlights that curve as if swathing bent knees. On the backside, create several curving vertical swaths of highlighting that start just below where the scarf edges touch the dark robe. Extend the strokes down, feathering them out to end before reaching the bottom of the rock. You may prefer to sketch on guidelines first with a white pencil.

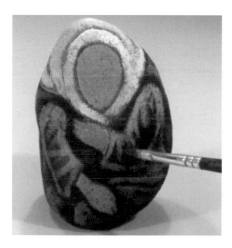

7 Soften Contrasts on Robe

Use a color like Summer Sky Blue, one that is lighter than the base color of the robes but darker than the robe's highlights, to soften the contrast between those two extremes. Use it sparingly along the sides and lower areas wherever highlights meet the darker base coat. Avoid the upper edges and sides where the highlights would be strongest.

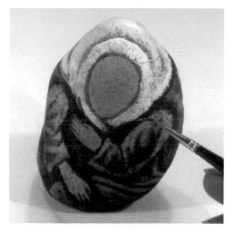

8 Paint Dark Details

Switch to a liner brush and black paint to reinforce and define the main folds and wrinkles in Mary's robes and to ensure that the arms, hands and fingers are all clearly defined.

9 Paint Skin Tones

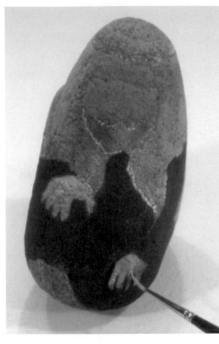

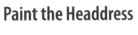

Mix more flesh color for Joseph's face and hands as well as the ankle and foot that show. A second coat may be needed for good coverage.

10 Fill in the Beard

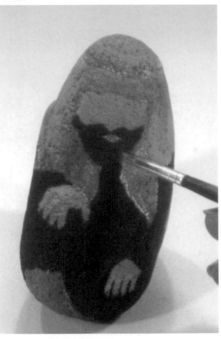

Mix Patio Brick with less black paint than you used on Joseph's robes and use this lighter shade of brown to fill in his beard. Leave the mouth unpainted.

11 Paint the Tunic

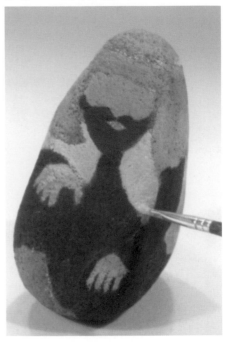

Rinse your brush and use Sunflower Yellow to paint Joseph's tunic. The open front resembles a vest but is longer in back and on the sides.

12 Paint the Headdress

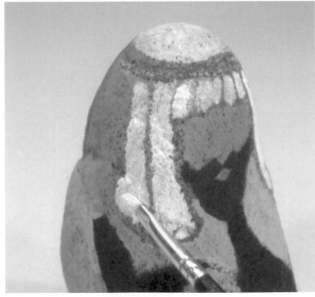

Use your small shader and white paint to fill in Joseph's headdress, leaving narrow lines of gray undercoating showing to serve as folds and gathers below the headband. Leave gray edges in place to outline the headdress for definition.

13 Highlight the Robes

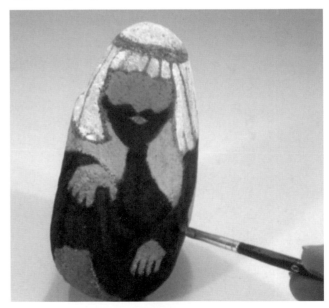

To create the look of soft folds and draping material on Joseph's robes, use Patio Brick and a small shader brush to highlight the upper edges of the sleeves. Paint several layers of curving folds draping down along either side of the raised knee and below both hands.

14 Paint Mary's Features and Add Shadows

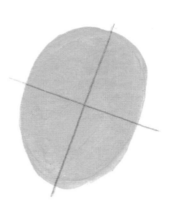

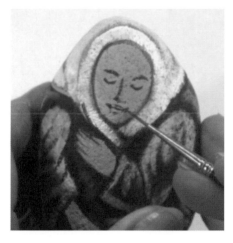

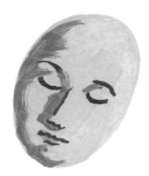

To place Mary's features, bisect the face oval as shown, with guidelines corresponding to the angle of the head, if it is tilted.

Use a liner brush and Patio Brick darkened with a tiny amount of black. Mix in just enough water to ensure the paint flows easily off the brush tip. Paint on Mary's delicate features.

Once the features have dried, add enough Patio Brick to the flesh tone to darken it. Use a small flat or round brush to shadow the features along one side to give them more dimension.

15 Paint Joseph's Features and Add Shadows

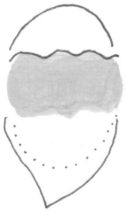

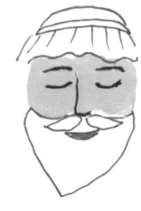

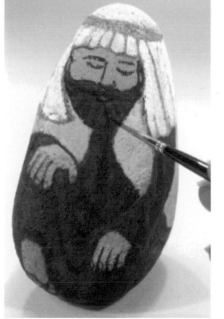

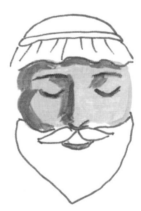

Fill in the face   *Paint on the features*

Shadow the features

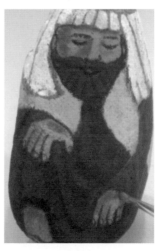

Use your liner and a darker mixture of Patio Brick and black to add simple features to Joseph's face including a smiling mouth showing in his beard. Outline his hands and add a small round nail to each fingertip. Give his beard some detail by radiating narrow lines out below the mouth. Use this dark brown to redefine any folds, edges or features that are not clear. Darken flesh tone with Patio Brick and use it to shadow the face. Add shadows to the top of the hands below the sleeve openings and to the ankle below the robe's hem as shown.

16 Final Touches for Mary

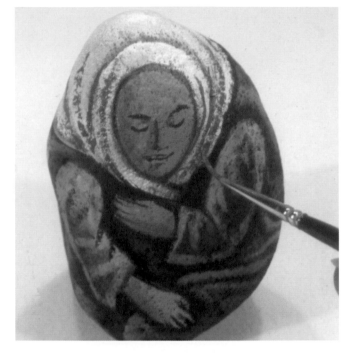

Mix up a bit of gray paint and use a clean liner brush to add delicate lines like shadowed folds along the lower half of Mary's scarf on either side of her face.

17 Paint Joseph's Foot Details

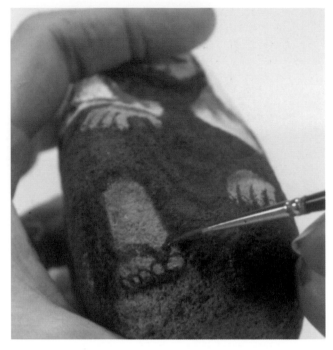

Fill in the space around the ankle and foot below the hem of Joseph's robe with black then mix in Patio Brick. Use a liner brush to paint toes and a add a simple sandal strap above them.

18 Highlight Tunic

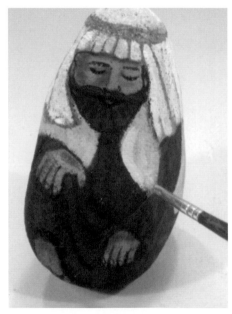

Lighten Sunflower Yellow with enough white to get a clearly paler shade and use it to highlight the center and edges of Joseph's tunic in front as well as along the edges in back.

19 Add Shadows to Tunic

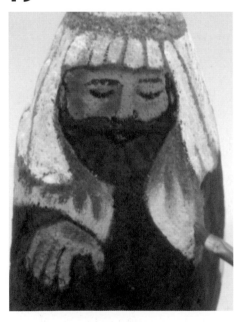

Tip: You can't 'ruin' a rock! If you aren't happy with the way something looks, simply paint over it and try again

Rinse your brush then darken a small amount of Sunflower Yellow with just enough black paint to make a yellowish-gray shade. Use this to paint shadows that begin around Joseph's beard and come down in soft folds between the highlights. On the backside, add a narrow band of shadows just below the hem of the headdress, along with a few folds on the back of the tunic.

20 Final Touches for Joseph

Choose a color to fill in Joseph's headband. I used Summer Sky Blue, but red is nice, too. Look for areas or features that need more definition and use dark brown paint and a liner brush to help them stand out. Even though the back sides are not a focal point, make sure they have a finished look.

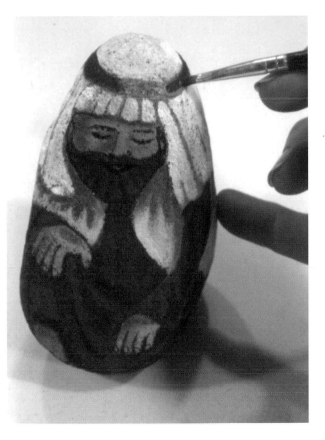

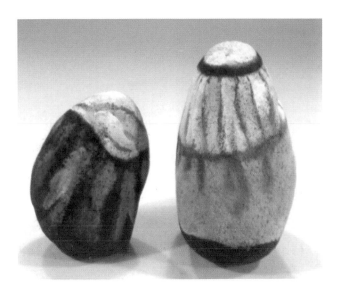

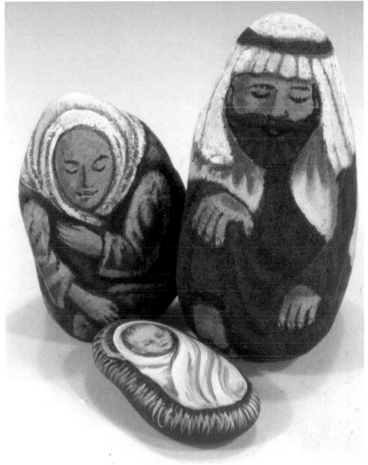

This set of figures is small but if you have access to large rocks and paint them with weather-resistant paint, (then seal them with Krylon for added protection), you would have a set suitable for display in your yard

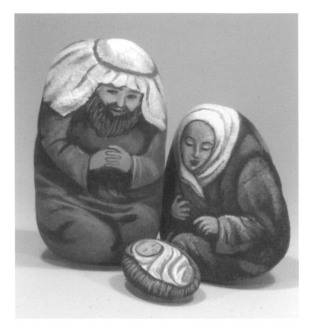

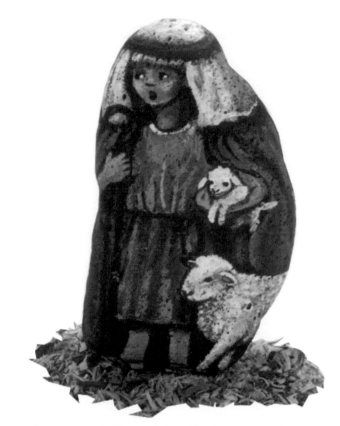

Changing the clothing colors gives this set a completely different look. Joseph's rock lent itself to having him kneeling on both knees

The curve of this rock inspired me to tuck a lamb under my shepherd's draping cloak

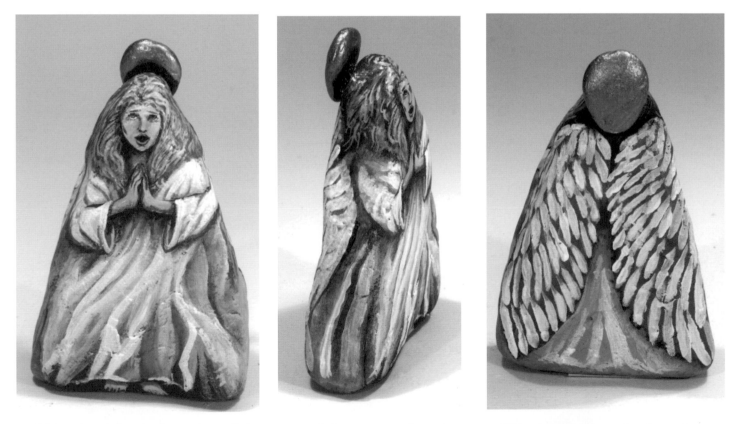

This triangular rock works well for an angel, but many other shapes could be used by changing how the wings are portrayed. I glued a pebble on for her golden halo and used a blue base coat to set off the folds of her flowing white gown. On the back there was ample room for a set of folded wings

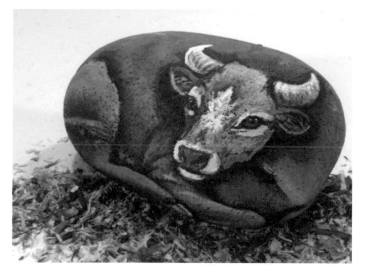

Use a plump oval rock to paint a gentle ox for the stable. I used shades of Patio Brick darkened with black or lightened with Sunflower Yellow.

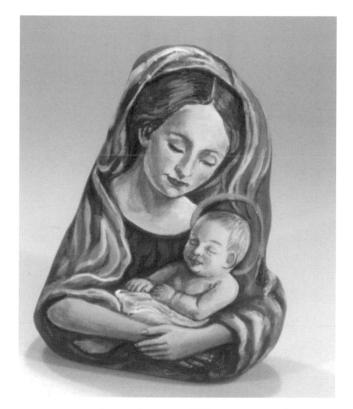

As you acquire painting skills you may discover many more ways to portray The Madonna and Child on various sizes and shapes of rocks

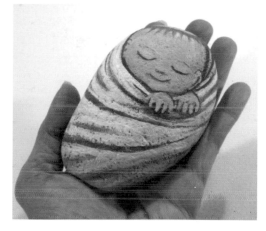

The Holy Infant could be as basic and simple as this example. Larger rocks are easier for young painters to handle

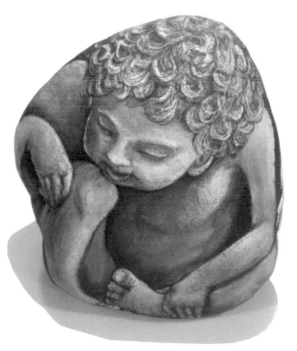

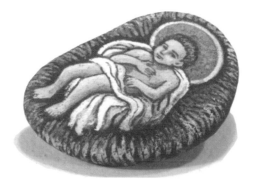

Classical paintings and classically inspired Christmas cards can provide the inspiration for more ornate versions

This chubby cherub rock has wings in back. A Christmas card image helped me see how to paint it in the style of Italian masters

Index

Hooked on Rock Painting?

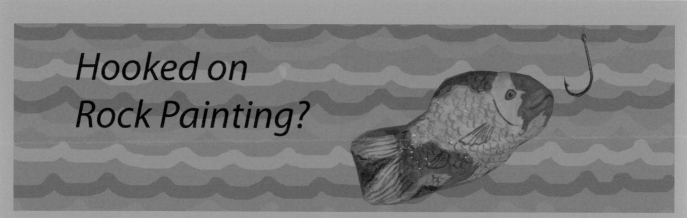

Leave no stone unturned! Explore Lin Wellford's other exciting books and video to discover even more fun and exciting ways to transform ordinary rocks into art!

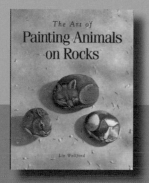 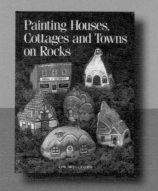 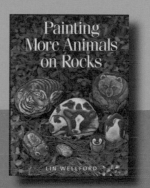 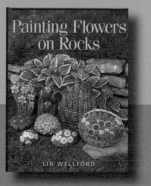

Start with lady bugs and turtles and work your way through an array of wildlife, cats, kittens and more!

Charming houses and cottages are among the easiest projects for new painters and loads of fun to make.

Frogs, penguins, mice, tigers, bears and other animal projects plus many more ideas to challenge and inspire.

Anyone can have a green thumb with painted flowers and plants. Paint your own bloomin' rock gardens.

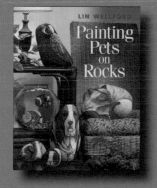 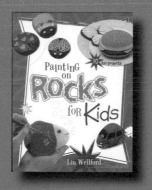 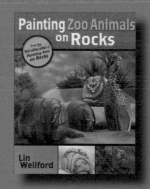 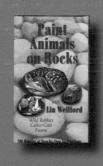

Paint three dimensional portraits of your favorite pets! A selection of dogs, cats, birds and fish plus examples of exotic pets.

Kids love to paint rocks! They'll learn basic techniques and develop hand-eye coordination, too.

Animal lovers go wild for these exotic creatures. Learn to build additions that add even more realism.

Watch Lin as she demonstrates her popular techniques for painting lifelike animals. Three complete projects- over 100 minutes.

Autographed copies are available through Lin's web site, www.LinWellford.com. Also available at book stores as well as craft and hobby stores, or call North Light Books (800) 289-0963
See the next page for details on ordering by mail.

Rock Painter's Resources

The supplies needed for painting rocks are common and should be easy to find. If you are unable to locate products in your area, contact the manufacturers listed below for help finding a retailer near you.

Brushes
Loew-Cornell, Inc.,
400 Sylvan Avenue,
Englewood Cliffs, NJ 07632
(201) 836-7070
www.loew-cornell.com

Paints
DecoArt Patio Paint
P.O. Box 386,
Stanford, KY 40484
www.decoart.com

Wood Filler
Leech's Real Wood Filler
P.O. Box 2147.
Huchinson, KS 67504
(800) 992-9018
www.leechadhesives.com

Liquid Nails
925 Euclid Ave.,
Cleveland, OH 44115
www.liquidnails.com

E6000 Craft Adhesive
www.E-6000.com

More Resources:
Yahoo Rock Painting Group
A free web club where rock painters exchange tips and show off their work.
www.groups.yahoo.com/group/rockpainting

Sign up for Lin's E-Newsletter at www.LinWellford.com or Email her at:
Lin@linWellford.com

Postal Book and Video Ordering information

Rock Painting Fun for Everyone! (96 pages)	$19.99
Painting on Rocks for Kids (64 pages)	$12.99
The Art of Painting Animals on Rocks (128 pages)	$22.99
Painting Houses, Cottages and Towns on Rocks (128 pages)	$22.99
Painting More Animals on Rocks (128 pages)	$22.99
Painting Flowers on Rocks (128 pages)	$22.99
Painting Pets on Rocks (128 pages)	$22.99
Painting Zoo Animals on Rocks (128 pages)	$22.99
Paint Animals on Rocks with Lin Wellford Video (100 mins.)	$19.99

(Add postage charges below to all orders)

Postage on any one item $2.75. Two or more items, add $2.00 each
(Prices subject to change- if they go up, you will be contacted)

Mail to: ArtStone Press, 210 E. Main, Green Forest, AR 72638